BRIDGE BASICS 2

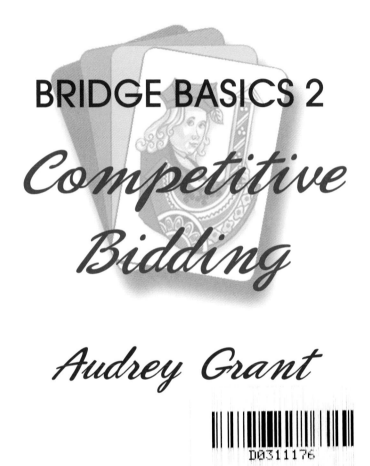

Competitive Bidding

Audrey Grant

Published by
Baron Barclay Bridge Supplies

REVISED EDITION

Bridge Basics 2: Competitive Bidding

Copyright © 2005 Audrey Grant's Better Bridge Inc.

If you'd like to contact the author, see page 229.

Baron Barclay
3600 Chamberlain Lane, Suite 230
Louisville, KY 40241
U.S. and Canada: 1-800-274-2221
Worldwide: 502-426-0410
FAX: 502-426-2044

www.baronbarclay.com

ISBN 0-939460-91-2

THIRD PRINTING

Illustrations by Kelvin Smith
Design and composition by John Reinhardt Book Design

Printed in the United States of America

Contents

Contents

Contents

The Bridge Basics Series

The Improving Your Judgment Series

... more to come

Introduction

The BRIDGE BASICS SERIES uses Audrey Grant Standard, a modern approach that is played in most games online, at tournaments, in golf clubs, on board ships, and among friends playing at home. The advisory committee for this system consists of the best players in the world.

BRIDGE BASICS 2—COMPETITIVE BIDDING covers the information needed when both partnerships are bidding during the auction. We still want to get to our best contract, but we also try to make it as difficult as possible for the opponents to reach their best spot. We need a more aggressive style of bidding: to bid more with less! This book introduces innovative methods of hand valuation and the bids that experts use in competitive situations.

There's one more step. The best way to absorb information is to use it. The thirty-two carefully prepared deals in this book provide an opportunity to practice. They put the bidding into a meaningful context and advance our play of the hand and defensive skills. Audrey's Coded Cards are available (see next page) to simplify dealing the hands.

I'm confident that the information in this book will give you what you need to play a good, enjoyable game of bridge—when both sides are competing!

All the best,
Audrey Grant
www.AudreyGrant.com

Audrey's Coded Cards

For each book in the Basic series there is a companion deck of color-coded cards available (see page 230) which is designed to make it easy to deal and play all thirty-two practice deals.

To use the cards, place the guide card that accompanies the deck in the center of the table.

Distribute each of the cards according to the color-coding on the back. To distribute Deal #7, for example, look at the box numbered 7 on the back of each card. If the box is red, the card goes to North; if it is blue, the card goes to East; yellow goes to South; green goes to West.

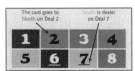

Check that each player has thirteen cards. The dealer is indicated by an underline of the number in the box. It is also indicated on the guide card. The deal is then ready to be bid and played...and replayed as often as desired.

If you are practicing by yourself, turn all four hand face up on the table, dummy style and walk through the bidding and play, using the text as a guide where necessary.

If you don't have the color-coded cards available, sort a deck of cards into suits and construct the four hands one suit at a time.

Have Fun!

Acknowledgments

To my husband, *David Lindop*, a world-class player who works hand-in-hand with me to produce the bridge books.

To *Jason Grant-Lindop* and *Joanna Grant* for their support and involvement in the many aspects of Better Bridge

To the Better Bridge Advisory Committee:
- *Bob Hamman* — World Champion, top-ranked male player
- *Petra Hamman* — World Champion, bridge teacher
- *Shawn Quinn* — World Champion, top-ranked female player
- *Fred Gitelman* — Founder of Bridge Base Inc., gold medalist
- *Henry Francis* — Editor, Official Encyclopedia of Bridge
- *Jerry Helms* — Professional bridge teacher and player

To the bridge teachers. Your dedication, skill, and professionalism have made me proud to be counted among you.

To the students of the game—thank you for sharing your ideas and your enthusiasm.

So far in our study of bidding technique we have been concerned solely with reaching our best contract. That is the proper objective when our side has most of the high cards, but when the position is reversed our aim must be to prevent the opponents from making the best of their cards. One way of achieving this is by opening with a bid of three or four in a suit.

Such bids are not strong in high cards, but are based on long suits of seven or eight cards. They are known as pre-emptive or shut-out bids. The idea is to put up a barrage high enough to shut the opponents out of the auction, or at least to make it hard for them to reach their best contract.

—HUGH KELSEY, START BRIDGE THE EASY WAY (1976)

Preemptive Opening Bids

The Concept of Preemptive Bids

Compare these two hands:

1) ♠ 6
   ♥ A K 7 4
   ♦ A K 8 3
   ♣ A K 8 6

2) ♠ K Q J 10 9 8 7
   ♥ 5
   ♦ 9 5 2
   ♣ 7 3

At first glance, they seem to have little in common. The first hand has 21 *high-card points* (HCPs); the second, only 6 high-card points. The first is at the top of the range for an opening bid at the *one level*; the second doesn't have enough *strength* to open 1♠.

Yet they do have something in common. Both hands have 6 *playing tricks*—tricks the hand can be expected to take if the partnership buys the *contract*. The first hand can be expected to take six tricks through the power of the *high cards*: the ♥A-K, ♦A-K, and ♣A-K. The second hand can take six tricks if spades are trumps, through the power of the long, strong spade suit.

Since both hands can take 6 tricks, it seems clear that both should qualify for an opening bid. However, the first hand meets the requirements for an opening bid at the one level, but the second does not since a 1♠ opening bid would describe a hand with about 13-21 points. To take advantage of hands that have a good, long suit but less than the values for an opening bid, the classic *preemptive opening bid* was introduced. With the second hand, opener would start with 3♠.

Why start the the bidding at the three level with a hand too weak to open at the one level? An opening bid in a suit at the three level describes a weak hand with the strength focused in one long suit and the potential to take about six tricks. The advantage of a preemptive opening bid is that it takes up a lot of room on the *Bidding Ladder* (see Appendix 3, on page 219) and makes it difficult for the opponents to get into the *auction* when they have the majority of the strength.

Consider East's dilemma if North opens 3♠:

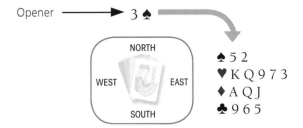

Opener ⟶ 3 ♠

NORTH

WEST   EAST

SOUTH

♠ 5 2
♥ K Q 9 7 3
♦ A Q J
♣ 9 6 5

With 12 high-card points plus 1 *length point* for the five-card heart suit, East was planning to open the bidding 1♥. After North opens 3♠, East is faced with a challenge. To bid hearts, East would have to start at the four level and bid 4♥. That might get the partnership much too high. If East passes, however, the partnership might miss a good contract. North's preemptive opening bid has made it more likely that East-West might bid too much or too little. It's for reasons such as this that preemptive bids have become an integral part of *competitive bidding*.

There are risks to making a preemptive bid. North's 3♠ opening makes it difficult for East to bid, but could also make it difficult for South, North's partner, to bid effectively. There is a danger North-South will be *defeated* in the 3♠ contract and will lose points to East-West. To understand how to balance the potential risks against the possible gains, it's necessary to consider the scoring.

Scoring

The format of the game—*rubber bridge, duplicate, Chicago*—affects the way the game is scored. A more detailed explanation is given in Appendix 1 (page 213) but here is an overview. Two factors impact the score for making or defeating a contract:

- Vulnerability
- Penalty Double

Vulnerability

In rubber bridge, a partnership that has not won a game is *non vulnerable* and a partnership that has won a game is *vulnerable*. In duplicate or Chicago scoring, the vulnerability is assigned on each *deal*.

The key point is that bonuses and penalties are higher when vulnerable than when non vulnerable.

Penalty Double

The side that doesn't win the auction can *double* the contract if it feels *declarer* can't make the required number of tricks. This is referred to as a *penalty double*. Doubles are discussed in more detail later in the book, but the key point is that a penalty double dramatically affects the size of the penalty if the contract is defeated.

You score points in three ways:

- Trick Score
- Bonus Points
- Penalty Points

Trick Score

The points for making a contract are calculated as follows:

- 20 points per trick bid and made in clubs or diamonds, the *minor* suits.
- 30 points per trick bid and made in hearts or spades, the *major* suits.
- 40 points for the first trick and 30 points for each subsequent trick in notrump.

If declarer makes a contract of 2♥, for example, the trick score is 60 points (30 + 30). A contract of 3NT is worth a trick score of 100 points (40 + 30 + 30).

Game is a total trick score of 100 or more points. Game can be scored in a single deal by bidding and making the following *game contracts*:

3NT (nine tricks)	40 + 30 + 30 = 100
4♥ or 4♠ (ten tricks)	30 + 30 + 30 + 30 = 120
5♣ or 5♦ (eleven tricks)	20 + 20 + 20 + 20 + 20 = 100

Bonuses

The bonuses awarded depend on the format of the game. In duplicate bridge, for example, the bonuses for bidding and making contracts are:

- 300 for bidding and making a non vulnerable game contract.
- 500 for bidding and making a vulnerable game contract.
- 50 for bidding and making a partscore contract.

For bidding and making a non vulnerable 3NT contract, the partnership would receive a trick score of 100 (40 + 30 + 30) plus a game bonus of 300, for a total of 400. If the partnership is vulnerable, the trick score is 100 plus a game bonus of 500, for a total of 600.

Bonuses are discussed in more detail in Appendix 2, but a key point is that the value of bidding and making a game is approximately 500 points.

Penalty Points

If declarer doesn't make the required number of tricks, the opponents receive points for each trick by which contract is defeated[1]. The penalty depends on the vulnerability and whether the contract is doubled.

If the contract is *undoubled* the penalty is:

- Non vulnerable: 50 points per trick.
- Vulnerable: 100 points per trick.

If the contract is doubled, the penalty is:

- Non vulnerable: 100 points for the first trick, 200 points for the second and third trick, and 300 points per trick thereafter.
- Vulnerable: 200 points for the first trick and 300 points per trick thereafter.

It is more costly to be defeated (*go down*), when vulnerable and the penalty rapidly increases if the contract is doubled, as can be seen from the following chart:

	Undoubled		Doubled	
	Non vulnerable	Vulnerable	Non vulnerable	Vulnerable
Down 1	50	100	100	200
Down 2	100 (50+50)	200 (100+100)	300 (100+200)	500 (200+300)
Down 3	150 (50+50+50)	300 (100+100+100)	500 (100+200+200)	800 (200+300+300)

Notice that the penalty for being defeated three tricks, doubled and non vulnerable or two tricks doubled and vulnerable is 500 points, about the value of bidding and making a game contract.

---

[1] The score for making a doubled contract is detailed in the Appendix.

The Guideline of 500

When you make a preemptive bid, you are expecting to be defeated in the contract if the opponents hold the majority of strength. The hope is that the penalty for being defeated will be less than the value of the potential contract the opponents could make.

Deliberately *overbidding* to a contract you don't expect to make is referred to as a *sacrifice*. You are hoping to sacrifice some scoring points to the opponents in exchange for the larger score they could get in their best contract.

Estimating the value of the opponents' potential contract is a challenge since it depends on whether the contract is in notrump, a major suit, or a minor suit, whether their side is vulnerable, and the scoring format (rubber, duplicate, Chicago). However, a useful guideline to keep in mind is the value of making a game contract is approximately 500 points.

When you are preempting to try to prevent the opponents from making a game contract, you don't want to get a penalty of more than 500 points since that is the approximate value of their game[2]. Since they can double for penalties, you don't want to overbid by more than two tricks vulnerable or three tricks non vulnerable. If you are defeated two tricks doubled and vulnerable, the penalty is 500 points (200 + 300); if you are defeated three tricks doubled and non vulnerable, the penalty is 500 points (100 + 200 + 200).

Although this is a guideline, it is often referred to as the *Rule of 500* or the *Rule of Two and Three*. In essence, it says that you need to be a little more cautious about preempting when your side is vulnerable.

---

[2] If you occasionally lose 800 or more points on a given deal, you're in good company. The best players in the world have stories about being defeated for a large number.

Three-Level Preemptive Opening Bids[3]

Estimating the number of playing tricks a hand is worth and taking into account factors such as vulnerability can be quite challenging. So, most players use some straightforward guidelines for deciding when to make a preemptive opening bid.

For a preemptive opening bid in a suit at the three level, the guideline is:

Three-Level Preemptive Opening

An opening bid of 3♣, 3♦, 3♥, or 3♠ shows:
- A long suit   Usually seven or more cards with two of the top three or three of the top five cards in the suit.
- A weak hand   Less than the values for an opening bid at the one level.

A good seven-card suit translates into about 6 or 7 playing tricks if the contract is played with the long suit as the trump suit. Having most of the strength concentrated in the long suit makes it quite likely the opponents can make a game contract in one of the other suits or in notrump if partner can't provide more than one or two tricks.

A preemptive opening bid serves two purposes. It is an *obstructive bid*, designed to make it more difficult for the opponents to enter the bidding and find their best contract. It is also quite descriptive, helping *responder* decide How High and Where the partnership belongs.

---

[3]Preemptive opening bids can also be made at the four level or higher, typically with an eight-card or longer suit.

Examples

The following hands meet the requirements for a three-level pre-emptive opening:

♠ K Q J 10 9 8 7   3♠. There are only 6 high-card points plus
♥ 6   three length points, not enough to open 1♠.
♦ 8 5 2   The seven-card spade suit is strong with
♣ 7 3   four of the top five *honors*. The hand has
                     6 playing tricks—the only spade trick the
                     opponents can take is the ♠A.

♠ 6   3♥. The heart suit isn't quite as good but
♥ A Q J 9 8 7 4   there are three of the top five honors. With
♦ 8 3   only 7 high-card points plus 3 length points
♣ 9 4 2   for the seven-card suit, there is not enough
                     strength to open 1♥. 3♥ describes the
                     hand well and will make the auction more
                     challenging for the opponents if they have
the majority of the strength.

The playing strength is more of a challenge to estimate but there are probably still at least six tricks with hearts as trumps. The opponents are likely to take only the ♥K, or they may take no heart tricks if partner has the ♥K or if the ♥K can be trapped.

♠ 8 6   3♦. This hand barely qualifies for a
♥ 4   preemptive opening. Although the diamond
♦ K J 10 9 8 7 3   suit has three of the top five honors, there
♣ J 10 5   are only 5 high-card points, putting this on
                     the low end of the scale. It's possible the
                     opponents could win the ♦A and ♦Q, so
                     there could be only five playing tricks.

It is with a borderline hand like this that you might want to consider the vulnerability when deciding whether to open 3♦. If your side is non vulnerable, you would probably choose to open 3♦ since the penalty is not as large if you are doubled. If your side is vulnerable, you might choose to be more cautious and pass, since the penalty for being defeated is larger, especially if the contract is doubled for penalty.

The following hands would not meet the requirements for a preemptive opening bid at the three level.

♠ J 8 7 6 4 3 2
♥ K J 5
♦ A 7
♣ 6

Pass. The quality of the seven-card suit isn't good enough for a three-level opening bid. There is no guarantee of taking more than three or four tricks with spades as the trump suit. This hand illustrates the importance of having a good suit for a preemptive opening. With only 9 high-card points, there isn't enough strength to open at the one level.

♠ 4
♥ A K J 9 8 5 3
♦ 7 3
♣ K J 5

1♥. With a good seven-card suit and 12 high-card points plus 3 length points for the seven-card suit, there is enough strength to make an opening bid at the one level. Preemptive opening bids describe hands unsuitable for an opening bid at the one level.

Responding to Three-Level Preemptive Opening Bids

An opening preemptive bid at the three level is very descriptive: a good seven-card suit but fewer than 13 points. Opener has five or six playing tricks in the trump suit. Responder can use this information to decide How High and Where the partnership belongs.

Responder's decision focuses on playing tricks, rather than high-card points. Sometimes responder can immediately choose the contract. At other times, more information is needed. After a preemptive opening bid, responder can pass, *raise* opener's suit, bid a *new suit*, or bid notrump. Let's look at each in turn.

Pass

When opener starts with a preemptive bid, opener is hoping partner, the responder, has at least two cards in the trump suit. If responder doesn't have three or more trumps, it is usually best to pass unless responder can picture enough tricks for a game contract. For example, suppose North opens the bidding 3♠ and East passes. It's South's *call*.

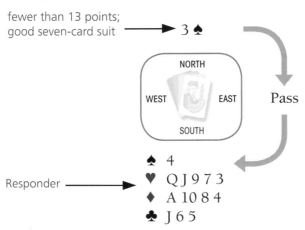

fewer than 13 points; good seven-card suit ⟶ 3 ♠

NORTH

WEST EAST Pass

SOUTH

Responder ⟶
♠ 4
♥ Q J 9 7 3
♦ A 10 8 4
♣ J 6 5

Pass. South doesn't like North's choice of spades as the trump suit, but bidding will only get the partnership higher on the Bidding

Ladder. North's spades will be longer and stronger than South's hearts. Since South can contribute only one *sure trick*, the ♦A, South should pass and leave North to try to take nine tricks with spades as trumps.

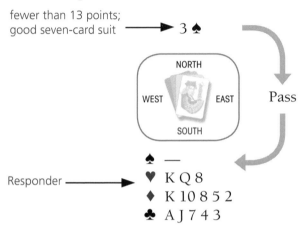

fewer than 13 points;
good seven-card suit ⟶ 3 ♠

NORTH

WEST   EAST   Pass

SOUTH

♠ —
Responder ⟶ ♥ K Q 8
♦ K 10 8 5 2
♣ A J 7 4 3

Pass. North probably has no more than six playing tricks and South, even with 13 high-card points plus 1 point for the length in diamonds and 1 point for the length in clubs, can't contribute enough tricks to make a game contract. Don't consider playing in notrump with no *fit* for partner's suit. North will get several tricks with spades as the trump suit, but may be unable to provide a single trick in a notrump contract. There may be no way to reach North's hand.

Raising the Preemptive Opening

There are two quite different reasons for raising the preemptive opening bid when responder has three-card or longer *support* for opener's suit. First, responder may have enough strength that the partnership can likely make a game contract. For example, suppose North opens 3♠, East passes, and it's South's call.

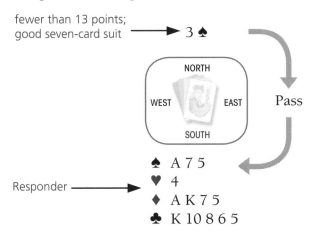

fewer than 13 points;
good seven-card suit ⟶ 3 ♠

NORTH

WEST   EAST   Pass

SOUTH

♠ A 7 5
Responder ⟶ ♥ 4
♦ A K 7 5
♣ K 10 8 6 5

4♠. With three-card support for North's spades, South expects North to have a good chance of taking ten tricks. South counts three sure tricks, the ♠A and ♦A-K. There is also a chance that North will be able to trump a second round of hearts with a small spade in the South hand—the dummy—to gain a trick. North may even be able to trump more than one heart in the dummy. So, the partnership should go for the game bonus. North has about six playing tricks and South can likely contribute four tricks, for a total of ten tricks.

There is another reason to raise opener's preemptive bid. There may be so little combined strength that it is likely the opponents can make a game or even a *slam* contract. With three or more cards in opener's suit, responder might want to raise to make it more challenging for the opponents to reach their best contract.

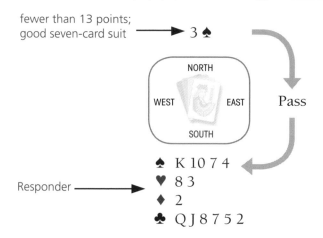

fewer than 13 points;
good seven-card suit ⟶ 3 ♠

NORTH

WEST   EAST   Pass

SOUTH

♠ K 10 7 4
Responder ⟶ ♥ 8 3
♦ 2
♣ Q J 8 7 5 2

4♠. Here South raises to game out of weakness rather than strength. South doesn't expect the partnership to take ten tricks. However, since North has shown a weak hand with little or no strength outside the spade suit, it's likely the opponents can make at least a game contract and maybe a slam if given enough room to find their best spot. By raising to 4♠, South hopes to take away more bidding room from the opponents.

Even though the 4♠ contract will probably be defeated, the opponents' score is likely to be less than the score they would get for bidding and making their game or slam contract. South is making a sacrifice.

Bidding a New Suit

If responder can determine How HIGH and WHERE the partnership belongs, responder can simply bid to the appropriate contract. For example, responder can make a *signoff* bid by bidding a game in another suit.

If responder is unsure How HIGH or WHERE the contract belongs, responder needs to make a *forcing* bid to get more information from opener. A new suit bid below game is forcing even in competition. Opener must bid again. Since opener is already promising a good seven-card suit, responder will usually have a good six-card or longer suit to suggest an alternative trump suit and be able to imagine a game. For example:

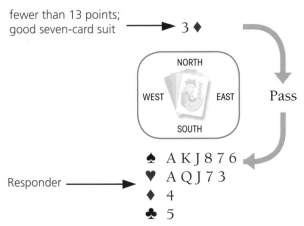

fewer than 13 points;
good seven-card suit ⟶ 3 ♦

NORTH

WEST   EAST   Pass

SOUTH

♠ A K J 8 7 6
Responder ⟶ ♥ A Q J 7 3
♦ 4
♣ 5

3♠. Despite North's preemptive opening bid, South wants to look for a fit in a major suit. South responds 3♠. When South bids a new suit, North can raise with support or *rebid* the original suit without support. If North rebids 4♦, South plans to bid 4♥ next, hoping North will have support for one of the suits.

Bidding No Trump

It's rare for responder to choose a notrump contract after an opening preemptive bid. It's often difficult to get to partner's hand unless the long suit is trump because entries are a problem.

The Weak Two-Bid

Like the three-level preemptive opening bid, the weak two-bid is primarily an obstructive bid, designed to make it more difficult for the opponents to enter the bidding and find their best contract. However, it is also quite descriptive, helping responder decide How HIGH and WHERE the partnership belongs.

For a preemptive opening bid in a suit at the two level, the guideline is:

Two-Level Preemptive Opening (Weak Two-Bid)

An opening bid of 2♦, 2♥, or 2♠ shows:
- A six-card suit   Usually two of the top three or three of the top five cards in the suit.
- 5–11 high-card points   Less than the values for an opening bid at the one level.

The main difference between a weak two-bid and a three-level preemptive opening is that a weak two-bid is typically made with a six-card suit and a three-level preempt is made with a seven-card suit. Also, weak two-bids can be opened only in diamonds, hearts, and spades, not clubs[4].

Examples

The following hands meet the requirements for a weak two-bid:

♠ 7
♥ K Q J 10 9 8
♦ 10 7 3
♣ 9 6 2

2♥. This is an ideal hand for a weak two-bid opening. There are only 6 high-card points plus two length points, not enough to open 1♥. The solid heart suit will produce five playing tricks with hearts as the trump suit.

---

[4]The 2♣ opening bid is used to show a very strong hand of about 22 or more points. This is covered in BRIDGE BASICS 3—POPULAR CONVENTIONS.

♠ A J 10 9 7 3
♥ 4 2
♦ 7 4
♣ J 5 2

2♠. The suit has three of the top five honors and the hand has only 6 high-card points. Opening 2♠ describes the hand well and makes the auction more challenging for the opponents if they have the majority of the strength. It's a challenge to estimate the number of playing tricks, but the hand could be expected to take at least four, and maybe five, tricks.

♠ 8 6
♥ Q 5 2
♦ Q J 10 8 7 3
♣ 7 6

2♦. This hand barely qualifies for a weak two-bid. There are only 5 high-card points, putting this on the low end of the scale. The suit does have three of the top five honors, but you wouldn't want to have much less. Missing the ♦A and ♦K, you could expect only four playing tricks.

Here are hands that would not meet the requirements for a weak two-bid.

♠ 10 8 6 5 4 3
♥ A 10 3
♦ 8 6
♣ K J

Pass. The suit quality isn't good enough for a weak two-bid although there is a six-card suit. With only 8 high-card points, you would pass. There is no guarantee of taking more than two or three tricks with spades as the trump suit and the hand has some potential trick-taking value on *defense*.

♠ 4 2
♥ K 7 2
♦ A K J 9 7 3
♣ J 8

1♦. There is a good six-card suit and enough strength to make an opening bid at the one level, 12 high-card points plus 2 length points for the six-card suit.

♠ 10 9 5
♥ 7
♦ J 7 3
♣ A Q 10 8 7 5

Pass. With a reasonable six-card suit and less than the values for a one-level opening bid, the hand appears suitable for a weak two-bid. However, an opening bid of 2♣ is reserved to show a very strong hand.

Responding to a Weak Two-Bid

An opening weak two-bid is very descriptive, showing a good six-card suit but less than the values for an opening bid at the one level. It describes a hand with four or five playing tricks. Responder uses this information to decide How High and Where the partnership belongs. Responder's decision is based on the trick-taking potential of the *combined hands* rather than high-card points.

The responses are similar to those after a three-level preemptive opening. Responder can pass, raise opener's suit, or bid a new suit. In addition, responder has a special bid, 2 NT, that can be used to obtain more information.

Pass

Without support for partner's suit, the situation is similar to responding to a three-level opening preemptive bid. It is usually best to pass unless responder has enough strength that a game contract is still a possibility. For example, suppose North opens the bidding 2♠, East passes, and it's South's call.

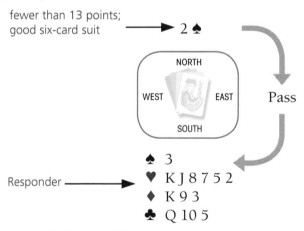

fewer than 13 points;
good six-card suit ⟶ 2 ♠

Pass

Responder ⟶
♠ 3
♥ K J 8 7 5 2
♦ K 9 3
♣ Q 10 5

Pass. South doesn't like partner's choice of spades as the trump suit but, if South bids, the partnership gets higher on the Bidding Ladder with no guarantee of a better landing spot. North's spades are likely to be as good as or better than South's hearts. North has at most about five playing tricks and South can't contribute enough for game to be a possibility. Responding to a preemptive opening is not the same as responding to an opening bid at the one level.

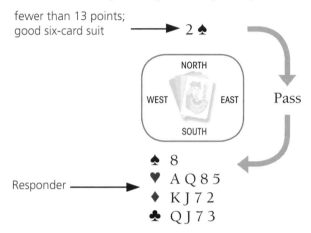

fewer than 13 points;
good six-card suit ⟶ 2 ♠

Pass

Responder ⟶

♠ 8
♥ A Q 8 5
♦ K J 7 2
♣ Q J 7 3

Pass. South has enough to open the bidding but not the values to take the partnership any higher after North's 2♠ bid. North has less than the values for an opening bid—and only four or five playing tricks—so there won't be enough combined strength to consider going for a game bonus. The only sure trick South can provide is the ♥A. High cards such as the ♥Q, ♦K-J, and ♣Q-J, might provide a couple of tricks, but there is no guarantee. Hopefully, South has enough strength that North can take eight tricks in the 2♠ contract.

South shouldn't consider playing in notrump with no fit for partner's suit. North's six-card suit will take several tricks if spades are trumps, but won't provide many tricks in a notrump contract. Even if South could *establish* some winning tricks in partner's spade suit, there would be difficulty getting to them. North will have little or no strength outside the spade suit.

Raising the Preemptive Opening

The weak two-bid is preemptive. The reasons for raising partner's suit are similar to those for raising a three-level preemptive bid:

- Responder may have enough strength that the partnership can likely make a game contract.
- Responder may have so little strength that it is likely the opponents can make a game or even a slam contract. With a fit for partner's suit responder might want to raise to make it more challenging for the opponents to reach their best contract.

For example, suppose North opens with a weak 2♥ bid, East passes, and South, as responder, has to decide How HIGH and WHERE.

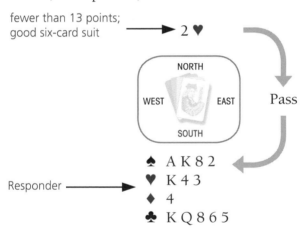

fewer than 13 points;
good six-card suit ⟶ 2 ♥

NORTH

WEST　　　EAST　　Pass

SOUTH

Responder ⟶
♠ A K 8 2
♥ K 4 3
♦ 4
♣ K Q 8 6 5

4♥. With three-card support for North's hearts, South can go for the game bonus because there should be a good chance of taking ten tricks. The ♠A, ♠K, ♥K, and ♣K-Q combination should each provide a trick. In addition, North may be able to gain a trick or two by trumping diamonds in the South hand, the dummy, since South has only one diamond.

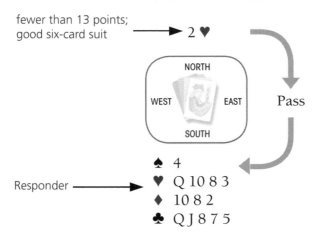

fewer than 13 points;
good six-card suit ➤ 2 ♥

NORTH

WEST   EAST   Pass

SOUTH

♠ 4
Responder ➤ ♥ Q 10 8 3
♦ 10 8 2
♣ Q J 8 7 5

4♥. Here South jumps to game for a completely different reason. South doesn't expect the partnership to have enough combined strength to take ten tricks. However, since North has shown a weak hand with little or no strength outside the heart suit, it's likely the opponents can make at least a game contract and maybe a slam if given enough room to find their best spot.

By jumping to 4♥, South hopes to take away even more bidding room from the opponents. Even though the contract will probably be defeated by several tricks, the opponents' score is likely to be less than the score they would receive for bidding and making their game or slam contract.

Bidding a New Suit

If responder is unsure How High or Where the contract belongs, responder needs to make a forcing bid to obtain more information from opener. A response in a new suit is forcing, showing a five-card or longer suit. Opener can raise with support or rebid the original suit without support. For example:

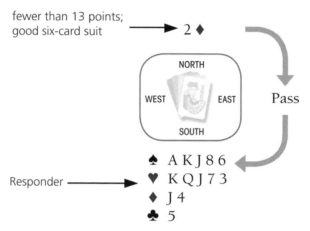

fewer than 13 points; good six-card suit → 2♦

Pass

Responder →

♠ A K J 8 6
♥ K Q J 7 3
♦ J 4
♣ 5

2♠. If North can't support spades and rebids 3♦, South can bid 3♥, showing the second suit. If North doesn't like hearts either and rebids 4♦, South can put the partnership in game in 5♦. Hopefully, the only tricks lost will be a club and a heart.

The Special Meaning of a 2NT Response

A response of 2NT to a weak two-bid has a special—*conventional*—meaning. It asks opener for a further description of the hand. It is used only when responder can imagine a game if opener has a 'good' weak two-bid.

With a minimum weak two-bid of about 5-8 points, opener simply rebids the suit at the three level. With more than a minimum, opener can bid a new suit to show a *feature* in that suit, such as an ace or king, or bid 3NT with a solid suit but no outside feature.

Here is an example of using the 2NT response to obtain more information:

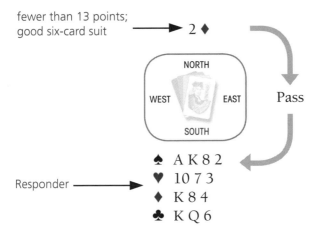

fewer than 13 points;
good six-card suit → 2♦

Pass

Responder → ♠ A K 8 2
♥ 10 7 3
♦ K 8 4
♣ K Q 6

2NT. South has enough to try for game. If North shows a minimum weak two-bid by rebidding 3♦, South can pass and settle for partscore. If North bids 3♥, for example, showing a maximum with the ♥A or ♥K, South can bid game. 3NT is likely to be easier than 5♦.

Declarer's Plan—The ABC's[5]

When the auction is over, the *opening lead* is made and dummy is placed face up on the table, declarer should make a plan for taking enough tricks to make the contract. There are three suggested stages, the ABC's:

Declarer's Plan—The ABC's

Assess the Situation
Browse Declarer's Checklist to Develop Extra Tricks
Consider the Order

Assess the Situation

This stage can be divided into three steps:

1) **Goal.** Start by considering the number of tricks required to make the contract. In 4♥, for example, declarer needs to take ten tricks.

2) **Sure Tricks[6].** Count the sure tricks, or *winners*—those that can be taken without giving up the lead. An ace is a sure trick; an ace and king in the same suit are two sure tricks.

3) **Extra Tricks Needed.** Compare the number of tricks needed to the sure tricks. If there are eight sure tricks in a contract of 4♥, for example, two more are needed.

---

[5] This is a review of play concepts introduced in the first book of the series. A more detailed discussion is in the book on DECLARER PLAY.

[6] In a trump contract, declarer can also count *losers*—the tricks that could be lost to the defenders. This is discussed in more detail in the book on DECLARER PLAY.

Browse Declarer's Checklist to Develop Extra Tricks

When there aren't enough sure tricks to make the contract, declarer looks at the various techniques for developing, or establishing, extra tricks:

Declarer's Checklist	
Promotion	
Length	
The Finesse	
Trumping in Dummy	

The first three methods are available in both notrump and trump contracts. The fourth is available only in trump contracts.

PROMOTION

Declarer can sometimes turn cards into winners by driving out the higher-ranking cards. For example:

DUMMY
♥ 4 2

DECLARER
♥ K Q

Declarer can lead the ♥K, or ♥Q, to drive out the defenders' ♥A and promote the remaining high card into a winner.

LENGTH

If declarer continues to lead a suit until the defenders have no cards left, declarer's remaining cards in the suit become winners.

DUMMY
♦ 9 6 3

DECLARER
♦ A K 7 5 2

Declarer can take two sure tricks with the ♦A and ♦K and then lead a third round of diamonds, giving up a trick to the defenders. If the five missing diamonds are divided 3-2, declarer's two remaining diamonds are winners.

In predicting how many tricks can be developed from a suit through length, declarer can use the guideline:

An odd number of missing cards tends to divide
as evenly as possible; an even number of missing cards
tends to divide slightly unevenly.

So, when five cards are missing, declarer can expect them to divide evenly, 3-2. If six cards are missing, declarer can expect them to divide slightly unevenly, 4-2. There is no guarantee when developing tricks through length. Five missing cards could be divided 4-1 or 5-0. Six missing cards could be divided 3-3, 5-1, or 6-0.

THE FINESSE

Declarer can sometimes develop tricks with high cards when the defenders hold higher-ranking cards.

DUMMY
♠ A Q

DECLARER
♠ 7 6

The ♠A is a sure trick, but the ♠Q is not since the defenders have the ♠K. However, declarer can hope to take two tricks by leading a low spade toward dummy and playing—finessing —dummy's ♠Q. If the ♠K is favorably placed on declarer's left, the ♠Q will win. If the ♠K is unfavorably placed on declarer's right, the finesse will lose and declarer will get only one trick.

A general guideline for taking finesses is to lead toward the card you hope will take a trick.

TRUMPING IN DUMMY

In a trump contract declarer can sometimes gain a trick by using dummy's trump.

Dummy	The trump suit is hearts. If declarer takes the
♥ 7 5 3	five heart winners and the ♣A, declarer gets
♣ 6	six tricks. If declarer plays the ♣A and then
	leads the ♣7 and trumps it in the dummy,
Declarer	declarer gets seven tricks: the ♣A, the *ruff*,
♥ A K Q J 10	and the five heart winners. Declarer gains a
♣ A 7	trick by trumping in the dummy.

Consider the Order

When developing and taking tricks, the order in which the tricks are played can be important. Here are some considerations:

1) **Take the tricks and run**. With enough sure tricks to make the contract, declarer should generally take them.

2) **Draw trumps**. In a trump contract, declarer should draw the defenders' trumps by playing the trump suit until the defenders have none left, unless declarer needs the trump suit for other purposes, such as trumping in dummy.

3) **Keep enough trumps in dummy**. When planning on trumping in dummy, declarer may have to delay drawing trumps to keep enough trumps in dummy.

4) **Develop extra tricks early**. To develop extra tricks, one or more tricks may have to be lost. Declarer should not be afraid to lose such tricks early, while keeping sure tricks in the other suits to regain the lead and then take the established winners.

5) **Be in the right place at the right time**. Declarer must often plan to be in the appropriate hand to take or establish winners.

6) **Play the high card from the short side first**. When taking sure tricks or promoting winners in suits that are unevenly divided between the hands, it's usually a good idea to start by playing the high cards from the hand with the fewer cards.

SUMMARY

Requirements for a Three Level Preemptive Opening

- A good seven-card suit.
- Less than the values for an opening bid at the one level.

Requirements for a Weak Two-Bid Opening

- A good six-card suit in diamonds, hearts, or spades.
- 5–11 high-card points.

Responding to a Preemptive Opening

When responding to a preemptive opening, focus on the trick-taking potential of the combined hands instead of the high-card points.

- Pass with no fit for opener's suit and little prospect of making a game contract.
- Raise opener's suit in two situations:
  - When the partnership is likely to be able to take enough tricks to make a game contract.
  - When you have support for opener's suit but a weak hand and it is likely the opponents can make at least a game contract.
- When you are interested in reaching game but are unsure How High and Where the partnership belongs:
  - Bid a new suit (forcing) to see if opener has support.
  - Bid 2NT after a weak two-bid to ask for more information.

The Guideline of 500

When making a preemptive opening bid:

- Don't overbid by more than three tricks when non vulnerable.
- Don't overbid by more than two tricks when vulnerable.

Quiz – Part I

(For a) through s) refer to pages 3 and 4 or refer to the scoring summary in Appendix 2 on page 215.)

What is the trick score for bidding and making the following contracts:

a) 2♥?_____ b) 4♠?_____ c) 2NT?_____
d) 4♦?_____ e) 5♣?_____ f) 3NT?_____
g) Which of the above contracts would be game contracts?

What is the total score at duplicate bridge for bidding and making the following contracts when non vulnerable:

h) 3NT?_____ i) 4♠?_____ j) 5♦?_____

What is the total score at duplicate bridge for bidding and making the following contracts when vulnerable:

k) 3NT?_____ l) 4♥?_____ m) 2♠?_____

What is the penalty for being defeated the following number of tricks:

n) Down one trick, non vulnerable and not doubled? ___
o) Down two tricks, non vulnerable and doubled? ___
p) Down three tricks, non vulnerable and doubled? ___
q) Down two tricks, vulnerable and not doubled? ___
r) Down two tricks, vulnerable and doubled? ___
s) Down three tricks, vulnerable and doubled? ___

How many playing tricks are in each of the following hands?

t) ♠ A 8 5   u) ♠ 10 5   v) ♠ 3
   ♥ A 9 6   ♥ 7 3   ♥ A K J 10 9 8
   ♦ A K 6 5   ♦ K Q J 10 9 7 6 ♦ 9 5 4
   ♣ 9 7 3   ♣ 8 4   ♣ J 6 2

   ____   ____   ____

Answers to Quiz – Part I

a) 60 (30 + 30). Major suit contracts, hearts and spades, score 30 points per trick.

b) 120 (30 + 30 + 30 + 30).

c) 70 (40 + 30). Notrump contracts score 40 points for the first trick and 30 points per trick thereafter.

d) 80 (20 + 20 + 20 + 20). Minor suit contracts, clubs and diamonds, score 20 points per trick.

e) 100 (20 + 20 + 20 + 20 + 20).

f) 100 (40 + 30 + 30)

g) b), e) and f). Game contracts are those worth 100 or more points.

h) 400. Trick score of 100 (40 + 30 + 30) plus a 300 non vulnerable game bonus.

i) 420. Trick score of 120 (30 + 30 + 30 + 30) plus a 300 non vulnerable game bonus.

j) 400 Trick score of 100 (20 + 20 + 20 + 20 + 20) plus a 300 non vulnerable game bonus.

k) 600. Trick score of 100 (40 + 30 + 30) plus a 500 vulnerable game bonus.

l) 620. Trick score of 120 (30 + 30 + 30 + 30) plus a 500 vulnerable game bonus.

m) 110. Trick score of 60 (30 + 30) plus a 50 point partscore bonus.

n) 50. The penalty for being defeated non vulnerable and not doubled is 50 points per trick.

o) 300 (100 + 200). The penalty for being defeated non vulnerable and doubled is 100 for the first trick, 200 for the second and third tricks, and 300 per trick thereafter.

p) 500 (100 + 200 + 200).

q) 200 (100 + 100). The penalty for being defeated vulnerable and not doubled is 100 points per trick.

r) 500 (200 + 300). The penalty for being defeated vulnerable and doubled is 200 for the first trick and 300 per trick thereafter.

s) 800 (200 + 300 + 300).

t) Four. The ♠A, ♥A, and ♦A-K can be expected to take tricks.

u) Six. With diamonds as the trump suit, this hand can be expected to take six diamond tricks by driving out the missing ♦A.

v) Five. With hearts as the trump suit, this hand can be expected to take five tricks. One heart trick may have to be lost to the missing ♥Q.

Quiz – Part II

South is the dealer and neither side is vulnerable. What call would South make with the following hands?

WEST	NORTH	EAST	SOUTH
			?

a) ♠ 8 5
 ♥ 7 4
 ♦ 6 2
 ♣ K Q J 9 7 5 3

b) ♠ A J 10 8 7 5 3
 ♥ 6
 ♦ J 5 4
 ♣ 7 2

c) ♠ 5
 ♥ A Q 10 7 6 5 2
 ♦ K 4
 ♣ K 9 4

d) ♠ Q 4
 ♥ Q 9 3
 ♦ 9 8 7 6 4 3 2
 ♣ J

e) ♠ 9
 ♥ 3
 ♦ K J 10 8 7 5 4
 ♣ J 10 7 2

f) ♠ Q 10 9 7 5 4 3
 ♥ 8
 ♦ 8 7 5
 ♣ J 6

East-West are vulnerable and North-South are non vulnerable. North opens 3♥ and East passes. What call would South make?

WEST	NORTH	EAST	SOUTH
	3♥	PASS	?

g) ♠ K 9 7
 ♥ 4
 ♦ A J 8 2
 ♣ Q 10 7 5 3

h) ♠ A J 7 3
 ♥ K 9 4
 ♦ A K
 ♣ 7 5 4 3

i) ♠ K J 7 6 5 3
 ♥ —
 ♦ Q 10 8 3
 ♣ A 9 5

j) ♠ A Q 10 7 5 4 2
 ♥ 3
 ♦ K Q J
 ♣ A Q

k) ♠ 9 8 6
 ♥ Q 10 7 3
 ♦ 4 3
 ♣ K 9 7 6

l) ♠ K J 7 4
 ♥ 8
 ♦ K Q 6 2
 ♣ A J 7 5

m) ♠ 7
 ♥ K 6 3
 ♦ J 10 8 6 4
 ♣ Q 9 6 2

n) ♠ A Q 7 4
 ♥ A
 ♦ K Q 10 8 2
 ♣ A J 3

o) ♠ Q J 7 5
 ♥ 8 2
 ♦ K 9 6 4
 ♣ A 7 3

Answers to Quiz – Part II

a) 3♣. With a good seven-card suit and less than the values for an open-ing bid at the one level, South can open with a preemptive bid.

b) 3♠. The suit isn't solid but has three of the top five cards. South can expect to take five or six tricks with this suit so an opening bid of 3♠ is reasonable.

c) 1♥. South has a good seven-card suit but also has 12 high-card points plus 3 length points for the seven-card suit. With a hand that values 13 or more points, South opens at the one level.

d) Pass. South has a weak hand and a seven-card suit but the suit doesn't have any top honors. It would be too risky to open a preemptive bid.

e) 3♦. The diamond suit is good enough that it should provide at least five tricks even if South has to lose to the ♦A and ♦Q. The club suit might also provide a trick through length. Opening 3♦ is a practical bid.

f) Pass. This is a close decision. Some players might open 3♠ but it is risky with a suit of this quality. Still, it could work well.

g) Pass. South has only one sure trick. The partnership is high enough.

h) 4♥. North should have about six playing tricks. South's ♠A, ♥K, and ♦A-K should provide enough tricks to make game.

i) Pass. North should have more hearts than South has spades. Bidding is unlikely to improve the contract.

j) 3♠. North may have enough spades to raise. If not, North will rebid 4♥ and South can hope that is the best contract. 3♠ is forcing.

k) 4♥. With an excellent fit for hearts but little else, it is likely East-West can make a game or slam. South raises as a further preemptive action.

l) Pass. South's assortment of high cards might provide some tricks for North but unlikely enough to make a game.

m) 4♥. South doesn't expect to make 4♥ but it is likely East-West can make 4♠ or more. South's raise makes it more difficult for East-West.

n) 4♥. South doesn't have a lot of hearts but the hand should provide enough tricks for game. Notrump is unlikely to be successful since there may be no way to reach North's hand.

o) Pass. South has a little help but not enough to raise to game. South also has some potential tricks on defense if East-West decide to compete.

Quiz – Part III

Neither side is vulnerable. East passes. What call would South make with the following hands?

WEST	NORTH	EAST	SOUTH
		PASS	?

a) ♠ A Q J 10 9 5
   ♥ 6 4
   ♦ J 8 5
   ♣ 7 3

b) ♠ 5 3
   ♥ 7 4
   ♦ K Q 10 9 7 4
   ♣ Q 10 5

c) ♠ 8 5
   ♥ 7 3 2
   ♦ K 4
   ♣ A J 9 7 6 3

d) ♠ K Q 4
   ♥ K J 10 9 7 3
   ♦ A 9 2
   ♣ 6

e) ♠ K Q 10 9 7 6 4
   ♥ 5
   ♦ 8 7 4
   ♣ 7 3

f) ♠ 7 5
   ♥ Q J 9 7 6 3
   ♦ A 9 5
   ♣ 8 7

Both sides are vulnerable. North opens 2♥ and East passes. What call would South make with the following hands?

WEST	NORTH	EAST	SOUTH
	2♥	PASS	?

g) ♠ K J 7 3
   ♥ 6 4
   ♦ A Q 8 5 4
   ♣ Q 7

h) ♠ A K 8 4
   ♥ K 8 3
   ♦ 4
   ♣ K Q J 6 2

i) ♠ 3
   ♥ A J 7 5
   ♦ Q 3 2
   ♣ 10 8 7 5 2

j) ♠ A Q 8 7 6 3
   ♥ 5
   ♦ K J 4
   ♣ Q 9 6

k) ♠ A Q 8 4
   ♥ 3
   ♦ Q J 6 4
   ♣ K J 6 2

l) ♠ K Q J
   ♥ A 9 5
   ♦ J 8 3
   ♣ A 7 5 2

Answers to Quiz – Part III

a) 2♠. With 8 high-card points plus 2 length points for the six-card suit, South doesn't have enough to open at the one level but can open with a weak two-bid.

b) 2♦. With a good six-card suit and only 7 high-card points, South can open with a weak two-bid in diamonds to describe the hand.

c) Pass. Although South has a six-card club suit and not enough strength to open at the one level, South can't open a weak two-bid when clubs is the suit. South passes instead.

d) 1♥. South has a good six-card suit but, with 13 high-card points plus 2 length points, South can open at the one level.

e) 3♠. An opening of 3♠ is appropriate holding a good seven-card suit and less than the values for an opening bid at the one level.

f) Pass/2♥. This is a borderline decision since the quality of the heart suit is not ideal. Some players would open 2♥; others would pass. It would be easier if the ace were in hearts instead of diamonds.

g) Pass. Although South has enough strength to open the bidding—12 high-card points plus 1 length point for the five-card suit—there is unlikely to be enough combined playing tricks to make game.

h) 4♥. North should have about five playing tricks with hearts as the trump suit. South's hand should provide about five: two in spades, one in hearts, two in clubs and North may be able to ruff a diamond in the South hand.

i) 4♥. South doesn't expect to make 4♥ but, with such an excellent fit in North's suit and so little strength outside, South wants to make it more challenging for East-West to enter the auction.

j) Pass. South might prefer spades as the trump suit, but there's no guarantee South's spades are better than North's hearts. Also, a 2♠ response would be forcing, likely getting the partnership too high.

k) Pass. Since North is showing a hand too weak to open at the one level, it's unlikely there is enough combined strength for game. A notrump contract is unlikely to be successful since North will have little strength outside the heart suit.

l) 2NT. With enough strength to be interested in reaching a game contract, South can make use of the conventional 2NT response to get further information about North's hand. If North rebids 3♥ to show a minimum weak two-bid, South can pass and settle for partscore. If North bids anything else, South can go for the game bonus.

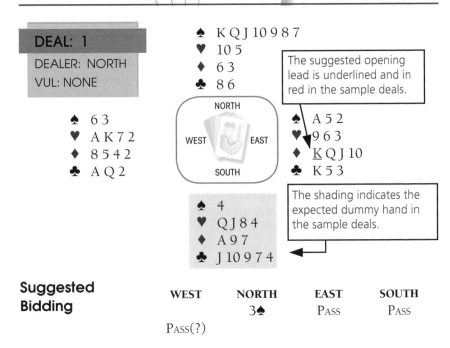

DEAL: 1

DEALER: NORTH
VUL: NONE

♠ K Q J 10 9 8 7
♥ 10 5
♦ 6 3
♣ 8 6

The suggested opening lead is underlined and in red in the sample deals.

NORTH
WEST   EAST
SOUTH

♠ 6 3
♥ A K 7 2
♦ 8 5 4 2
♣ A Q 2

♠ A 5 2
♥ 9 6 3
♦ K Q J 10
♣ K 5 3

The shading indicates the expected dummy hand in the sample deals.

♠ 4
♥ Q J 8 4
♦ A 9 7
♣ J 10 9 7 4

Suggested Bidding

WEST	NORTH	EAST	SOUTH
	3♠	Pass	Pass
Pass(?)			

North has only 6 high-card points plus 3 length points, not enough to open the bidding at the one level. With a good seven-card suit, however, North can make a preemptive opening bid of 3♠. This bid is obstructive, taking away a lot of bidding room from the opponents.

East has 13 high-card points, enough to open the bidding 1♦ but not enough to start competing at the three level or higher. North's preemptive 3♠ opening interferes with East's bid. East passes.

Although North's bid is obstructive, it is also descriptive. South knows the type of hand North holds. South doesn't like North's choice of trump suit, but knows that North has a good seven-card suit and wants to play with spades as trumps. With only one sure trick, the ♦A, South knows the partnership doesn't have enough combined strength for game and South passes.

West has 13 high-card points, enough to open at the one level. However, North's 3♠ opening has made it awkward for West to enter the auction. West may choose to pass[7]. That would end the auction.

[7] West might choose to enter the auction with a takeout double. This call is discussed in Chapter 3.

If North had passed instead of opening 3♠, East-West would likely get to a game contract of 3NT after an auction like this:

West	North	East	South
	Pass	1♦	Pass
1♥	Pass[8]	1NT	Pass
3NT	Pass	Pass	Pass

In 3NT, East has six tricks, the ♠A, ♥A-K, and ♣A-K-Q. East can promote three diamond tricks. Even if North can promote six spade winners, there is no way North can gain the lead to take them.

Suggested Opening Lead

East would lead the ♦K, top of the solid *sequence*, against North's 3♠ contract.

Suggested Play

North's goal is to take 9 tricks. There is only one sure trick, the ♦A. Eight more tricks are needed.

So, North moves to the second planning stage and browses Declarer's Checklist. North can plan to develop six winners in the spade suit through promotion. That will provide a total of seven tricks, two short of the goal, but that's the best declarer can do. The contract will be defeated two tricks.

```
┌─ DECLARER'S PLAN—THE ABC'S ─┐

  Declarer: North    Contract: 3♠

  ASSESS THE SITUATION
    Goal                  9
    Sure Tricks           1
    Extra Tricks Needed   8

  BROWSE DECLARER'S CHECKLIST
    Promotion          6 in spades
    Length
    The Finesse
    Trumping in Dummy

  CONSIDER THE ORDER
    • Draw trumps.
└─────────────────────────────┘
```

Conclusion

Being defeated two tricks in 3♠ is a good result for North-South. Since North and South are non vulnerable, the penalty is 100 points (50 per trick). That's much less than the score East-West would receive for bidding and making a game contract of 3NT. Even if North-South were doubled in the 3♠ contract, they would lose only 300 points.

[8] North might enter the auction at this point (see Chapter 2) but East and West are still likely to reach a game contract.

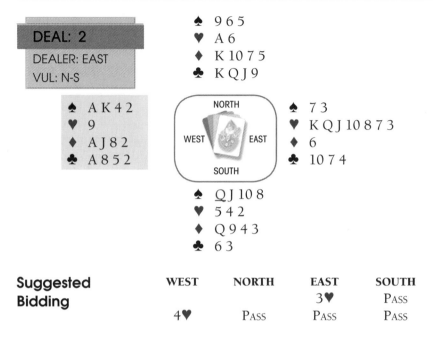

| **DEAL: 2** |
| DEALER: EAST |
| VUL: N-S |

North hand:
♠ 9 6 5
♥ A 6
♦ K 10 7 5
♣ K Q J 9

West hand:
♠ A K 4 2
♥ 9
♦ A J 8 2
♣ A 8 5 2

East hand:
♠ 7 3
♥ K Q J 10 8 7 3
♦ 6
♣ 10 7 4

South hand:
♠ Q J 10 8
♥ 5 4 2
♦ Q 9 4 3
♣ 6 3

Suggested Bidding

WEST	NORTH	EAST	SOUTH
		3♥	PASS
4♥	PASS	PASS	PASS

East has a good seven-card suit but not enough to open the bidding at the one level. Instead, East can start the auction with a preemptive opening bid of 3♥. East-West are non vulnerable and East's heart suit should produce six tricks.

South, with 5 high-card points, passes.

West knows that partner has a seven-card heart suit, so hearts should be a good trump suit even though West has only one heart. West also knows that East has about six playing tricks. With four sure tricks—the ♠A-K, ♦A, and ♣A—the partnership should be able to take ten tricks. West puts the partnership in the game contract of 4♥.

North, with 13 high-card points, doesn't have enough to enter the auction at the four level and passes. East and South have nothing more to say, so the auction is over.

Suggested Opening Lead

South would lead the ♠Q, top of the solid sequence, against East's 4♥ contract.

Suggested Play

After South makes the opening lead and the West hand comes down as the dummy, East makes a plan. As declarer, East's goal is to take at least ten tricks to make the 4♥ contract. East begins by counting the sure winners: two spades, one diamond, and one club for a total of four tricks. Six more tricks are required.

> **DECLARER'S PLAN—THE ABC'S**
>
> Declarer: East   Contract: 4♥
>
> **A**SSESS THE SITUATION
> | | |
> |---|---|
> | Goal | 10 |
> | Sure Tricks | 4 |
> | Extra Tricks Needed | 6 |
>
> **B**ROWSE DECLARER'S CHECKLIST
> - Promotion: 6 in hearts
> - Length
> - The Finesse
> - Trumping in Dummy
>
> **C**ONSIDER THE ORDER
> - Draw trumps.

Moving to the second stage, East browses Declarer's Checklist. The heart suit will provide six tricks through promotion once the ♥A is driven out.

After winning the first trick with one of dummy's high spades, declarer's priority is to draw the defenders' trumps. Declarer leads dummy's heart and continues leading hearts until the ♥A is driven out and the defenders have no trumps remaining. It is then safe for declarer to take the remaining winners.

Conclusion

West should not consider bidding 3NT with only one heart. East's hand is unlikely to produce many tricks in a notrump contract, but will provide a lot of tricks with hearts as the trump suit.

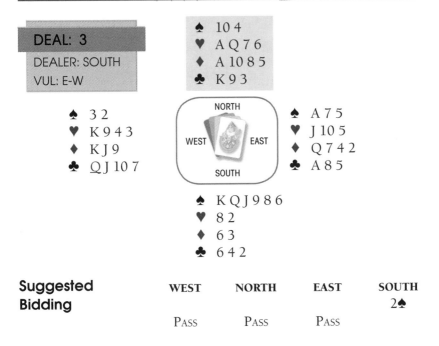

DEAL: 3

DEALER: SOUTH
VUL: E-W

NORTH
- ♠ 10 4
- ♥ A Q 7 6
- ♦ A 10 8 5
- ♣ K 9 3

WEST
- ♠ 3 2
- ♥ K 9 4 3
- ♦ K J 9
- ♣ Q J 10 7

EAST
- ♠ A 7 5
- ♥ J 10 5
- ♦ Q 7 4 2
- ♣ A 8 5

SOUTH
- ♠ K Q J 9 8 6
- ♥ 8 2
- ♦ 6 3
- ♣ 6 4 2

Suggested Bidding

WEST	NORTH	EAST	SOUTH
			2♠
Pass	Pass	Pass	

South is the dealer but, with 6 high-card points plus 2 length points, does not have enough to open the bidding at the one level. With a good six-card suit, however, South can open the bidding with a weak two-bid, 2♠. South is non vulnerable and has a reasonable expectation of taking five tricks with spades as trumps.

West has 10 high-card points and passes.

North has 13 high-card points, but knows there is unlikely to be enough combined strength for a game contract because South has shown less than the values for an opening bid. North passes.

East has 11 high-card points and passes, ending the auction. South becomes declarer in a contract of 2♠.

Suggested Opening Lead

With a solid sequence in clubs, West starts with the ♣Q, top of the touching high cards, against South's 2♠ contract.

Suggested Play

When the North hand is put down as the dummy, declarer makes a plan for playing the hand. South's goal is to take at least eight tricks. South can count on one sure trick in hearts and one in diamonds. That's a total of two tricks, six short of the goal.

South browses Declarer's Checklist for ways to develop the extra tricks. Five tricks can be promoted in the spade suit. Declarer can hope for an extra trick in hearts by trying the

---

DECLARER'S PLAN—THE ABC'S

Declarer: South   Contract: 2♠

ASSESS THE SITUATION

Goal	8
Sure Tricks	2
Extra Tricks Needed	6

BROWSE DECLARER'S CHECKLIST

Promotion:	5 in spades
Length	
The Finesse	1 in hearts
Trumping in Dummy	

CONSIDER THE ORDER

- Draw trumps.
- Be in the right place at the right time (to lead toward dummy's ♥Q).

---

finesse. If West holds the ♥K, declarer can lead toward the ♥Q, the card declarer hopes will take a trick.

After gaining the lead, declarer can start by leading spades. This has the two-fold effect of promoting winners in the spade suit by driving out the ♠A and of drawing trumps.

After trumps are drawn, it is time for the heart finesse. Declarer needs to be in the South hand to lead a low heart and finesse dummy's ♥Q. As long as West holds the ♥K, declarer will get a trick with both dummy's ♥Q and ♥A.

Conclusion

The weak two-bid immediately gets North-South to their best contract. If East-West enter the auction on this hand, they will get too high and North-South will score points by defeating their contract.

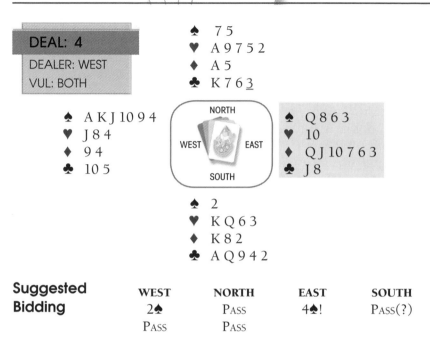

DEAL: 4

DEALER: WEST
VUL: BOTH

NORTH
♠ 7 5
♥ A 9 7 5 2
♦ A 5
♣ K 7 6 3

WEST
♠ A K J 10 9 4
♥ J 8 4
♦ 9 4
♣ 10 5

EAST
♠ Q 8 6 3
♥ 10
♦ Q J 10 7 6 3
♣ J 8

SOUTH
♠ 2
♥ K Q 6 3
♦ K 8 2
♣ A Q 9 4 2

Suggested	**WEST**	**NORTH**	**EAST**	**SOUTH**
Bidding	2♠	PASS	4♠!	PASS(?)
	PASS	PASS		

West doesn't have enough to open at the one level with only 9 high-card points and 2 length points. However, with a good suit and a reasonable expectation of taking five or six tricks with spades as trumps, West can open with a weak 2♠ bid.

North has 11 high-card points plus 1 length point for the five-card suit. North would have to bid at the three level to suggest hearts as trumps and that is too high. North passes.

East has only 6 high-card points but an excellent fit for spades. East can't expect the partnership to take more than seven or eight tricks, but that isn't the only consideration in deciding whether to pass or bid. West has shown a weak hand and East has so little strength it is very likely the opponents have enough strength for at least game. To make it more difficult for North-South to enter the auction, East can take additional preemptive action by jumping to 4♠!

South is now faced with a challenging decision on whether to enter the auction. With 14 high-card points plus 1 length point, South has enough to open at the one level but it might be dangerous to bid at the four level. South might choose to pass[9]. West and North will then pass, ending the auction.

Suggested Opening Lead

Against a trump contract, a low card is not usually led from a suit headed by an ace. So, North might choose to lead the ♣3, *fourth highest* in that suit. North might also consider leading the ♥A or ♦A.

Suggested Play

West's goal is to take ten tricks with spades as trumps. West counts six sure tricks in spades, but that's all. Four more tricks need to be developed.

Browsing Declarer's Checklist, there is an opportunity to get two extra tricks by trumping hearts in the dummy. Declarer will have to lose one heart trick first.

Suppose the defenders take the first two clubs and then lead a spade. Declarer can win and

---

DECLARER'S PLAN—THE ABC'S

Declarer: West   Contract: 4♠

ASSESS THE SITUATION

Goal	10
Sure Tricks	6
Extra Tricks Needed	4

BROWSE DECLARER'S CHECKLIST

Promotion
Length
The Finesse
Trumping in Dummy 2 in hearts

CONSIDER THE ORDER

- Draw trumps.
- Keep two hearts in dummy to ruff hearts.

---

play a second round of spades to draw the remaining trump, but shouldn't play any more trumps.

Instead, declarer gives up a heart trick. On regaining the lead, declarer can trump a heart in dummy. After getting back to the West hand, declarer can trump the remaining heart in dummy.

Conclusion

Being defeated two tricks in 4♠ is an excellent result for East-West. North-South can take twelve tricks with either hearts or clubs as the trump suit: five heart tricks, two diamonds, and five clubs. Even if the 4♠ contract is doubled, the penalty of 500 points for being defeated two tricks is less than the value of North-South's potential game or slam contract.

---

[9] South's options for entering the auction will be discussed in Chapter 3.

As many as ten factors may influence a player's decision to overcall. In roughly descending order of importance, they are:

- Suit length
- Strength
- Vulnerability
- Level
- Suit Quality
- Obstruction
- Opponents' skill
- Holding in opponent's suit
- Opponents' vulnerability
- Opponents' methods

—HENRY FRANCIS (EDITOR-IN-CHIEF),

THE OFFICIAL ENCYCLOPEDIA OF BRIDGE

Overcalls
and Advances

When both partnerships are bidding for the privilege of naming the trump suit or notrump, it is referred to as a *competitive auction*. One way to compete after the opponents open the bidding is to make a bid over an opponent's bid. This is referred to as an *overcall*.

An overcall and an opening bid have some similarities. You're making the first bid in the auction for your side and are trying to exchange enough information to choose the best contract. However, once both partnerships are competing for the privilege of naming the trump suit or notrump, the priorities for both sides can change. Let's take a closer look.

The Simple Overcall

East opens the bidding 1♦. What should South do?

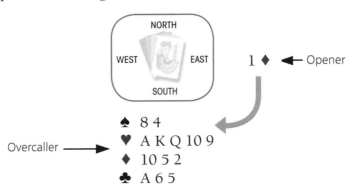

With 13 high-card points plus 1 length point for the five-card heart suit, South would have opened the bidding 1♥ if East had passed. South can still suggest hearts as a trump suit by making a 1♥ overcall.

Overcalling at the cheapest available level is a *simple overcall*. Here, South is making a simple overcall at the one level.

One difference between an overcall and an opening bid is that you can't always make an overcall at the one level. Suppose East had opened 1♠ instead of 1♦.

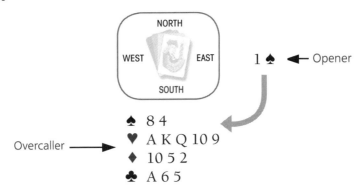

To suggest hearts as the trump suit, South would have to bid 2♥, a simple overcall at the *two level*.

Advantages and Risks of an Overcall

In competitive auctions, the goals change and this affects the requirements for making a bid. Consider South's call with this hand after East opens 1♣.

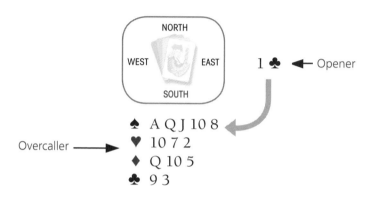

South would not open 1♠ with only 9 high-card points plus 1 length point for the five-card spade suit, but there are advantages to overcalling 1♠ with this hand:

- South wants to compete for the contract and prefers spades as trumps.
- A 1♠ overcall could interfere with the opponents' auction. Left to their own devices, the opponents usually settle into their best contract. The 1♠ overcall takes away room on the Bidding Ladder. For example, West can no longer respond 1♦ or 1♥. This may make it more difficult for the opponents to find their best trump fit and to stop at a comfortable level.
- If East-West win the auction, North-South will be defending. By overcalling 1♠, South may help the partnership find the best defense. If North has to make the opening lead, for example, South has suggested the spade suit.

There are also risks in overcalling:

- By overcalling, South gives information about the hand to the opponents as well as partner. This might help declarer make better decisions during the play if East-West win the auction.
- If South can't make 1♠, East-West will score points for defeating the contract. East has announced at least 13 points and West is in a good position to judge whether to bid higher or choose to defend and try to defeat the 1♠ contract. East-West could also double for penalties to increase the bonus the partnership receives if North-South can't make the contract.

Still, the advantages of overcalling tend to outweigh the risks, especially at the one level.

Guidelines for an Overcall

The guidelines for making an overcall try to balance the advantages and the risks. Here are some considerations[10]:

SUIT QUALITY

The longer and stronger your suit, the safer it is to overcall since you are less likely to be defeated by several tricks. Ideally, an overcall shows at least a five-card suit. If the suit is only five cards in length, it's safer to have two of the top three or three of the top five honors.

HAND VALUATION

When considering an overcall, the hand is valued the same way as for opening the bidding. Count high-card points—ace, 4; king, 3; queen, 2; jack, 1—and length points—1 point for a five-card suit; 2 points for a six-card suit; and so on.

LEVEL

The risk of overcalling at the one level is minimal compared to the advantages so, with a good suit, an overcall can be made with less

---

[10]Vulnerability is another consideration. You should be more cautious overcalling when vulnerable since the size of the penalty for being defeated is increased.

than the values for an opening bid. An overcall at the two level or higher, however, carries greater risk, so it tends to show a good suit and strength at least equivalent to that for opening the bidding.

The guidelines for making an overcall in a suit are:

The Overcall

Distribution: • A good five-card suit or a six-card or longer suit.

Strength: • 7 to 17[11] high-card points at the one level.
• 13 to 17 points at the two level or higher.

Examples

The following hands are suitable for an overcall by South after East opens 1♦.

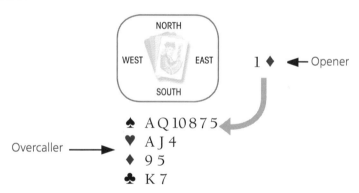

1♠. This is a very sound one-level overcall with 14 high-card points plus 2 length points for the six-card spade suit. South would open 1♠ as dealer. The overcall gets North-South into the auction.

---

[11] The upper range for an overcall is lower than that for the opening bid, about 17 points instead of 21. Occasionally, you have a good suit and a hand with 18 or more points. You would be disappointed if partner passed your overcall, so you prefer to make a stronger bid. This is discussed in Chapter 3.

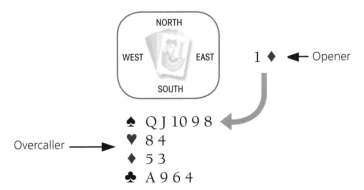

1♠. This is a minimum one-level overcall. There are only 7 high-card points and South would not open this hand. Still, there is a good five-card suit with three of the top five honors. South would take at least three spade tricks and the ♣A even if North has nothing. The risk in overcalling at the one level is minimal and South would like to compete, to interfere with the opponents, and to suggest a lead.

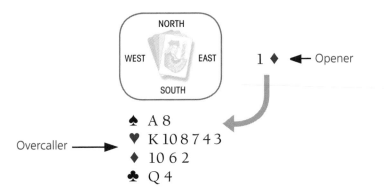

1♥. Although the hand is too weak to open the bidding if South were the dealer, there is enough strength for a one-level overcall. The sixth card in hearts makes up for not having three of the top five honors.

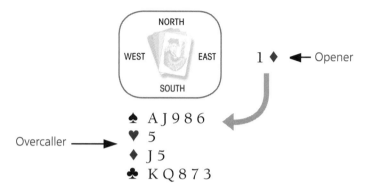

1♠. With two five-card suits, South overcalls the *higher-ranking*, the same choice as when opening the bidding. Although the spade suit does not have three of the top five honors, the second five-card suit provides compensation.

Simple overcalls at the two level or higher[13] require a good suit and approximately the values for an opening bid or more. Here are hands suitable for a two-level overcall.

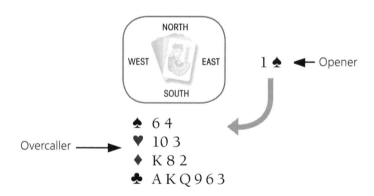

2♣. To overcall at the two level, South needs a good suit and about the same strength as for an opening bid. With 12 high-card points plus 2 length points for the six-card suit, this hand is strong enough to make a two-level overcall.

[13]See Practice Deal #30 for an example of an overcall at the three level.

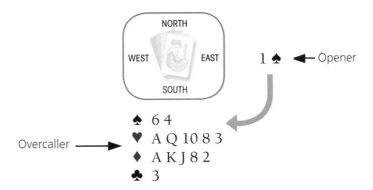

2♥. This is a good hand with enough strength to overcall at the two level. With a choice of suits to overcall, South chooses the higher-ranking.

Here are examples of hands for South that are unsuitable for making an overcall after East opens 1♥.

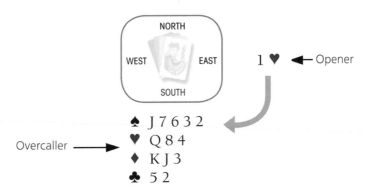

Pass. South has a five-card suit but, with a weak hand and a weak suit, there is little to be gained by overcalling. The risk of being defeated several tricks is substantial.

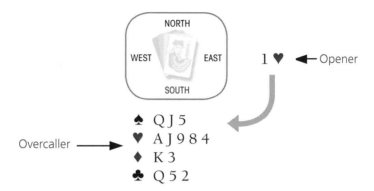

Pass. East picked the suit South likes best. South doesn't want to contest the auction in the same suit as East. Since South would be pleased to defend with hearts as trumps, there's no need to bid.

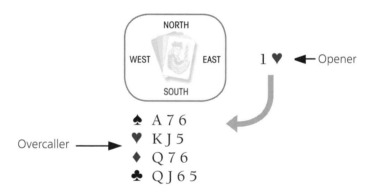

Pass. There is no five-card or longer suit to overcall. Even though South would open 1♣ with this hand, it's not necessary to overcall when an opponent opens the bidding. Passing can be a difficult call with 13 or more points, but it's a better choice than overcalling a weak four-card suit at the two level.

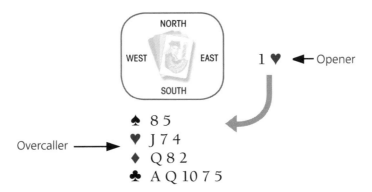

♥ ← Opener

♠ 8 5
♥ J 7 4
♦ Q 8 2
♣ A Q 10 7 5

Overcaller →

Pass. There is a reasonable five-card suit, but the hand isn't strong enough for a two-level overcall.

Making an Overcall After Both Opponents Have Bid

The overcall can be used after both opponents have bid. For example, suppose West opens 1♣, North passes, and East responds 1♥. It's South's call.

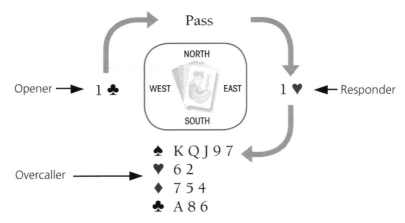

Opener → 1♣

1♥ ← Responder

♠ K Q J 9 7
♥ 6 2
♦ 7 5 4
♣ A 8 6

Overcaller →

1♠. Now is the time to enter the auction. South has a good five-card suit and 10 high-card points. Although both opponents have bid, North-South may still be able to make a contract. South doesn't want to leave the auction entirely to the opponents.

In this next example, West opens 1♠, North passes, and East raises to 2♠.

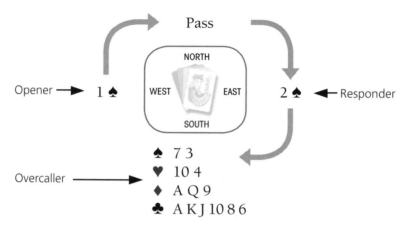

Pass

Opener ➝ 1♠   WEST   EAST   2♠ ⬅ Responder

	NORTH	
WEST		EAST
	SOUTH	

Overcaller ⟶
♠ 7 3
♥ 10 4
♦ A Q 9
♣ A K J 10 8 6

3♣. It's risky to come into the auction at the three level but, with a good six-card suit and a good hand, it's worth the chance. South doesn't want to let the opponents rest at a comfortable level in their chosen trump suit. Maybe South's 3♣ overcall will push East-West higher than they would like to be, or buy the contract.

Advancing a Simple Overcall

The partner of the opening bidder is the responder. The partner of the overcaller is referred to as the *advancer*.

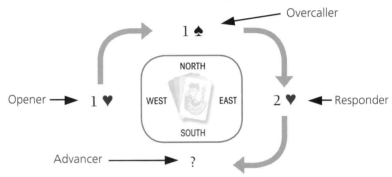

The different names are a reminder that the guidelines for an overcall are not identical to those for an opening bid. Consequently, the guidelines for advancing an overcall are not the same as those for responding to an opening bid. Fortunately, there are good reasons for the differences.

Advancer's Priority – Supporting Partner's Suit

An overcall, in either a major or a minor suit, shows a good five-card or longer suit and is a strong suggestion that this be the trump suit. Advancer's priority, therefore, is to show support with three or more cards in the suit. With support, advancer can value the hand using *dummy points: void – 5; singleton – 3; doubleton – 1.*

In a competitive auction, the purpose of raising partner's suit is two-fold:

- To try to reach your best contract. If your side has the majority of the strength you want to explore the possibility of game.
- To prevent the opponents from getting to their best contract. If your side doesn't have the majority of strength, the opponents are likely to win the auction and could get a game or even a slam. You want to bid to try to make it difficult for them to

find their best contract. By taking away room on the Bidding Ladder, the opponents may misjudge and bid too much or too little. It may be worthwhile to deliberately overbid—bid more than you think you can make. The advantage is that the penalty the opponents receive for defeating your contract may be less than their score for bidding and making their own contract.

SUPPORTING WITH MINIMUM VALUES

With three-card support for partner's overcalled suit and about 6–9 points, advancer can make a single—non-jump—raise. However, with a hand suitable for preemptive action—an *unbalanced* hand with four-card or longer support—advancer can make a jump raise to try to take bidding room away from the opponents.

As a guideline in competitive auctions, it is usually safe to raise to the level of the combined trumps held by the partnership[13]. For example: if the partnership has eight combined trumps, compete to the two level—eight tricks; if the partnership has nine combined trumps, compete to the three level—nine tricks; if the partnership has ten combined trumps, compete to the four level—ten tricks.

Since the overcaller promises at least a five-card suit, advancer can apply this concept to help decide HOW HIGH to raise a one-level overcall with fewer than 10 points:

Advancing a One-Level Overcall with Support and 6-9 Points

- 3-card support   Raise to the two level.
- 4-card support   Raise to the three level.
- 5-card support   Raise to the game level.

---

[13] This is based on The Law of Total Tricks, a theory popularized by Larry Cohen.

The jump raise to the three level or higher is referred to as a *preemptive jump raise*. With fewer than 6 points, advancer can simply pass[14].

The above chart is a guideline and advancer can exercise judgment. For example, advancer could choose to raise only to the two level with four-card support if the hand is *balanced*, the high cards are not in the trump suit, or the partnership is vulnerable.

Here are examples of advancing an overcall with support and about 6-9 points. West opens 1♥, North overcalls 1♠, and East raises to 2♥. It's South's call.

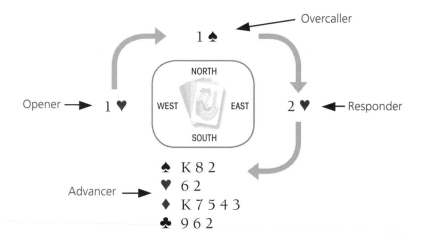

2♠. With three-card support for overcaller's spade suit and 7 points—6 high-card points plus 1 dummy point for the doubleton heart—South raises to the two level. South would bid 2♠ whether or not East passes.

---

[14]6–9 points is only a guideline. Some players will make a preemptive raise with fewer than 6 points.

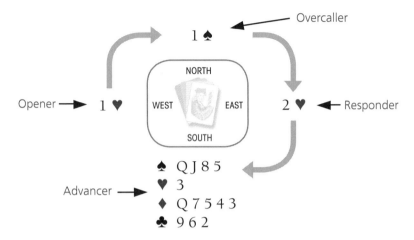

3♠. With four-card support for overcaller's spade suit and 8 points—5 high-card points plus 3 dummy points for the singleton heart—South makes a preemptive jump raise to the three level. If North has a minimum overcall and is defeated in this contract, it is likely that East-West can make a game contract and North-South have made a good sacrifice.

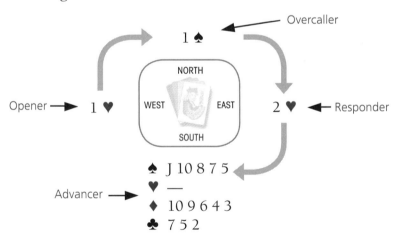

4♠. It may seem strange to jump to game with only a jack, but that's the recommended strategy for advancer with this type of hand. The hand is worth 6 points: 1 high-card point plus 5 dummy points for the heart void. North is unlikely to make 4♠, but it is very probable that East-West can make at least a game and maybe a slam.

For a two-level overcall, partner usually has the equivalent of an opening bid or better. There is less bidding room for the advancer but the options with 6-9 points are similar to those after a one-level overcall: a single raise shows three-card or longer support; a jump raise is preemptive showing four-card or longer support.

For example, West opens 1♠, North overcalls 2♥, and East raises to 2♠. It's South's call as advancer.

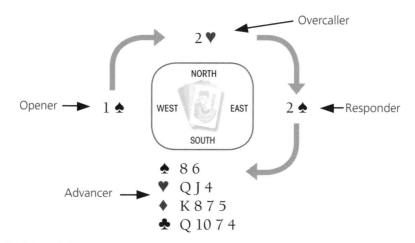

3♥. With 8 high-card points and three-card support for partner's heart suit, South has enough to raise, even though that will get the partnership to the three level. North has shown approximately the values for an opening bid or better by overcalling at the two level, so South wants to compete for the contract in the partnership's trump suit.

RAISING WITH 10+ POINTS–THE CUEBID

The situation is different when advancer has support and about 10 or more points. Your partnership could expect to make at least a partscore and maybe a game if partner has more than a minimum overcall. Rather than making it difficult for the opponents to reach their best spot, you're trying to reach your best contract.

A jump raise would describe a preemptive hand with 6-9 points and four-card support and might get the partnership too high. The solution is to make use of a bid that is available only in a competitive auction, the *cuebid*—a bid of the opponents' suit. For example, suppose West opens the bidding 1♦, North overcalls 1♠, and East passes. A bid of 2♦ by advancer, South, would be a cuebid.

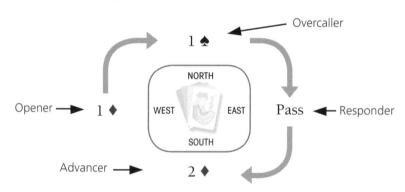

South's 2♦ bid is unlikely to be of much use in a natural sense. South would rarely want to play with diamonds as trumps once the opponents have bid diamonds. It is more practical to use a bid of the opponents' suit for other purposes. The cuebid becomes the tool for advancer to show a hand with support and interest in reaching a game contract, about 10 or more points.

Advancing an Overcall
with Support and 10+ Points

Cuebid the opponents' suit,
showing interest in reaching game.

The cuebid is forcing and the overcaller is expected to bid again if the opener passes. With a minimum, North, the overcaller, simply rebids the suit at the cheapest level. With more than a minimum, North makes some other descriptive bid such as a new suit or a jump in the overcalled suit. Advancer can then decide whether to stop in partscore or go for the game bonus.

Here are examples of South advancing an overcall with support and 10+ points after West opens 1♦, North overcalls 1♠, and East passes.

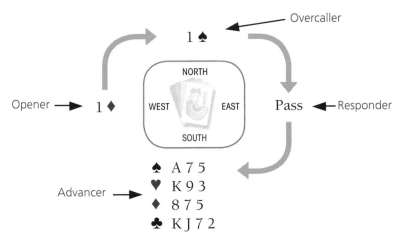

2♦. With three-card support for spades and 11 high-card points, South is too strong for a simple raise to 2♠. By starting with a 2♦ cuebid of the opponents' suit, South shows interest in reaching game. If North rebids 2♠, showing no extra strength, South will pass and the partnership rests in partscore at the two level.

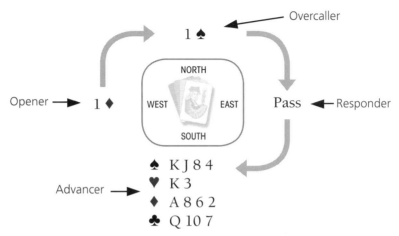

2♦. With four-card support for overcaller's suit and 14 points—13 high-card points plus 1 dummy point for the doubleton heart— South shows interest in reaching game by starting with a 2♦ cuebid. If North rebids 2♠, South can make a further try by raising to 3♠. The partnership can still stop short of game if North has a bare minimum overcall of about 7-10 points.

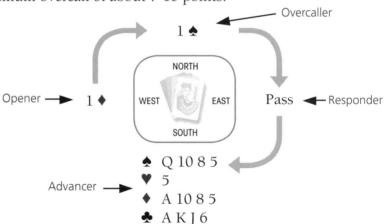

2♦. With four-card spade support and 14 high-card points plus 3 dummy points for the singleton heart, South starts with a cuebid. Even if North makes a minimum rebid of 2♠, South has enough to jump to 4♠. Why not jump to 4♠ right away? That would be a preemptive raise, showing a weak hand.

Advancer's Second Choice – A New Suit

Without support for overcaller's suit, advancer can consider bidding a new suit. Since the overcall has already suggested a good five-card or longer suit as the trump suit for the partnership, advancer should introduce another suit only if it is likely to be an improvement. Advancer can use the following guideline:

Guidelines for Advancing in a New Suit

- A good five-card suit or a six-card or longer suit.
- 6 or more points at the one level;
- 11 or more points at the two level.

A new suit response to an opening bid is forcing. An advance in a new suit is not forcing[15] since an overcall can be made with less than the values for an opening bid. The partnership doesn't want to get too high in a competitive auction when there isn't a good trump fit.

Here are examples of a new suit advance by South after West opens 1♣, North overcalls 1♥, and East passes.

---

[15]Some partnerships prefer a new suit advance to be forcing. Also, after a two-level or higher overcall, most partnerships would treat a new suit by advancer as forcing.

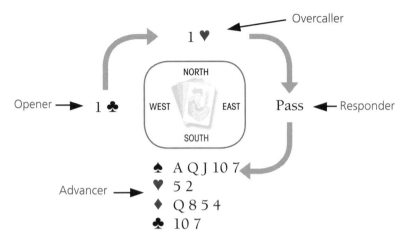

1♠. South doesn't have support for North's hearts but does have sufficient strength and a good enough suit to suggest spades at the one level. With a minimum overcall, North can pass South's change of suit to avoid getting too high[16].

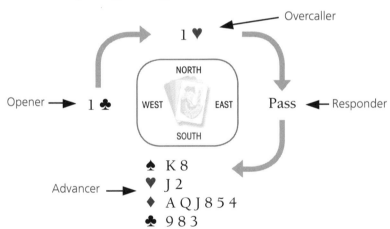

2♦. With 11 high-card points plus 2 length points for the six-card suit, South has enough to bid a new suit at the two level. North may pass with a minimum overcall but that should be fine. The partnership will be high enough.

[16] With a very strong hand where you would be disappointed if partner were to pass an advance in a new suit, you can start with a cuebid and then bid your suit.

Advancer's Third Choice – Notrump

With a balanced hand and some strength in the opponents' suit, advancer can bid notrump. For example:

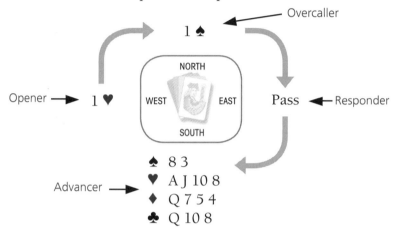

1NT. South doesn't have support for North's spades but does have 9 high-card points and some length and strength in hearts. South can suggest playing in notrump.

An advance of 1NT shows about 6–10 points; an advance of 2NT shows about 11–12 points. With 13 or more points, advancer will usually start with a cuebid.

Passing as Advancer

Advancer doesn't have to bid with no fit for partner's overcalled suit and no good suit to show.

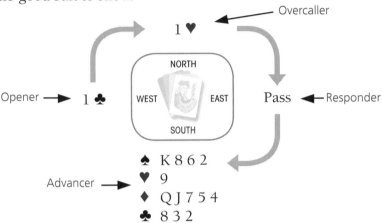

Pass. South has enough to respond if North had opened the bidding, But it's unlikely there is enough combined strength for game and any attempt to "improve" the contract may get the partnership further into trouble.

Rebids by the Overcaller

If advancer raises the overcalled suit, bids a new suit, or bids notrump, it's not forcing. The overcaller does not have to bid again. The overcaller can bid again with extra length in the overcalled suit or with a second suit to show. With extra values, the overcaller can move toward game or bid game.

If advancer cuebids, the overcaller must bid again. With nothing extra, the overcaller simply rebids the suit at the cheapest level. With more than minimum values, the overcaller can bid a new suit, jump in the overcalled suit, or bid notrump.

Rebids by the Overcaller after a Minimum Raise

The overcaller will usually pass advancer's simple raise. However, the overcaller may bid again with extra strength if it is possible there could be enough combined strength for game or if the opponents are also competing for the contract. For example, suppose you are West:

WEST	NORTH	EAST	SOUTH
			1♥
1♠	PASS	2♠	PASS
?			

♠	A Q 10 9 5
♥	8 5 4
♦	K 9 6
♣	J 5

Pass. There isn't enough combined strength for West to consider going for the game bonus level. West has 11 points—10 high-card points plus 1 length point for the five-card suit— and East's raise is showing about 6-9 points.

♠	A K 10 7 5 3
♥	Q 5
♦	A Q 6
♣	9 4

3♠. This is a strong overcall and there may be enough combined strength for game. If East has 8 or 9 points, East could bid 4♠. With 6 or 7 points, East can decline the invitation by passing.

In this next example, North-South compete to the three level in hearts:

WEST	NORTH	EAST	SOUTH
			1♥
1♠	2♥	2♠	3♥
?			

♠	A K J 10 5 3
♥	6 5
♦	A 9 6
♣	9 4

3♠. West has a choice of passing and defending against 3♥ or competing further. With a good six-card suit, competing to the three level seems reasonable.

Rebids by the Overcaller after a New Suit Advance

Advancer's new suit response is *invitational* but not forcing. With a minimum overcall, you can pass. With extra strength or *distribution*, you can bid again.

WEST	NORTH	EAST	SOUTH
			1♦
1♥	PASS	1♠	PASS
?			

♠ J 4 2
♥ K Q 10 9 5
♦ 9 6
♣ Q 8 2

Pass. East's new suit advance isn't forcing. East hasn't shown support for hearts and, with a minimum overcall, West passes and leaves the partnership to play partscore in spades.

♠ 3
♥ A Q J 9 7 5
♦ 10 5 3
♣ A 4 2

2♥. West doesn't have to bid again but, with a good six-card suit, wants to repeat the suggestion that the partnership play with hearts as the trump suit.

In this next example, opener bids again over East's advance.

WEST	NORTH	EAST	SOUTH
			1♦
1♥	PASS	1♠	2♦
?			

♠ A 10 4
♥ A J 10 7 5
♦ 5 4
♣ K 8 5

2♠. East didn't support West's hearts but West has support for East's spades. With more than a minimum overcall, West can compete further by raising spades.

Rebids by the Overcaller after a Notrump Advance

Advancer's response in notrump is not forcing. With a minimum hand, overcaller can pass. With extra strength or distribution, overcaller bids again.

WEST	NORTH	EAST	SOUTH
			1♣
1♠	PASS	1NT	PASS
?			

♠ K J 10 8 5
♥ A 9 3
♦ J 6 3
♣ 7 4

Pass. East didn't support West's spades and West has a minimum overcall. A partscore in notrump looks like the best spot.

♠ A Q 10 5 2
♥ 6 3
♦ K J 10 7 5
♣ 8

2♦. East didn't support spades, the first suggested suit. With an unbalanced hand unsuitable for notrump, West shows the second suit. East might prefer diamonds to spades.

Overcaller's Rebid after a Cuebid

Advancer's cuebid is forcing, showing interest in reaching game and asking for more information about the overcaller's hand. With a minimum, the overcaller rebids as cheaply as possible.

WEST	NORTH	EAST	SOUTH
			1♥
1♠	PASS	2♥	PASS
?			

♠ K Q J 8 3
♥ J 9 5
♦ Q 7 2
♣ 9 4

2♠. With nothing extra for the overcall, West rebids spades as cheaply as possible after East's cuebid, even though it is only a five-card suit.

With a medium-strength hand, the overcaller makes a forward-going bid: a new suit or a jump in the original suit.

WEST	NORTH	EAST	SOUTH
			1♣
1♥	PASS	2♣	PASS
?			

NORTH
WEST   EAST
SOUTH

♠ 8 3
♥ A K J 9 5
♦ K Q 7 2
♣ 9 4

2♦. West has a sound one-level overcall and interest in reaching game after advancer shows a good hand. West describes the hand further by showing the second suit.

With a maximum-strength hand, the overcaller takes the partnership to game.

WEST	NORTH	EAST	SOUTH
			1♦
1♠	PASS	2♦	PASS
?			

NORTH
WEST   EAST
SOUTH

♠ A K J 10 8 7 4
♥ 8 3
♦ 6
♣ A Q 9

4♠. Since advancer has about 10 or more points and interest in reaching game, West is willing to go for the game bonus after the cuebid.

The Notrump Overcall

Consider South's call with this hand after East opens 1♥:

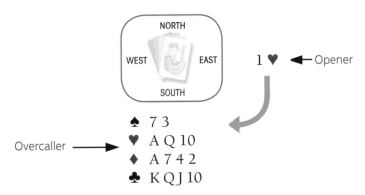

NORTH

WEST   EAST   1♥ ◄—Opener

SOUTH

Overcaller ——►
- ♠ 7 3
- ♥ A Q 10
- ♦ A 7 4 2
- ♣ K Q J 10

1NT. South would have opened 1NT if East had passed. An overcall of 1NT is similar to an opening bid of 1NT. It shows a balanced hand of about 15-17 points[17].

The only consideration is that East's 1♥ opening showed a five-card or longer suit and West is likely to lead a heart against South's notrump contract. So, South should have some strength in the opponents' suit to overcall 1NT.

---

[17] Since there is more risk in overcalling 1NT after an opponent has shown strength by opening the bidding, the range for a 1NT overcall is actually about 15-18 points. See Practice Deal #26 for an example of a 1NT overcall.

Since the 1NT overcall is similar to an opening bid of 1NT, advancer can bid in the same manner as responding to a 1NT opening bid. For example, suppose West opens 1♦, North overcalls 1NT, East passes, and it's South's call.

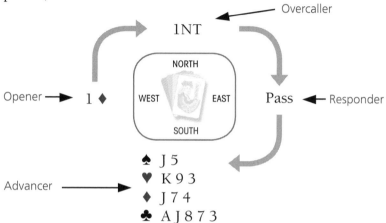

3NT. South has 10 high-card points plus 1 length point for the five-card suit. That's enough to take the partnership to game opposite North's 1NT overcall since the partnership has at least 26 combined points.

The Weak Jump Overcall

A *jump overcall*—bidding one or more levels higher than necessary—is similar to a preemptive opening bid. It shows a weak hand with a long suit[18]. Consider South's call with this hand after East opens 1♦:

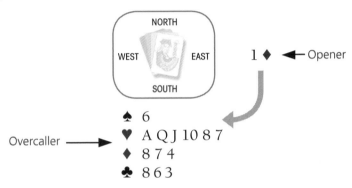

NORTH

WEST   EAST   1 ♦ ◄— Opener

SOUTH

♠ 6
Overcaller ——► ♥ A Q J 10 8 7
♦ 8 7 4
♣ 8 6 3

2♥. With a good six-card suit but a hand too weak to open at the one level, South would have opened 2♥, a weak two-bid, if East had passed. So, instead of making a simple overcall of 1♥, South can make a preemptive jump overcall of 2♥.

Like the weak two-bid, the advantage of the weak jump overcall is that it takes up room on the Bidding Ladder, making it more challenging for the opponents to find their best contract[19]. Since there is the risk of being doubled for penalty, the hand should be worth about five or six playing tricks.

---

[18] Some partnerships use a jump overcall to show a hand too strong for a simple overcall, but the popular modern style is to use weak jump overcalls.

[19] See Practice Deals #27 and #28 for examples of the effect of a weak jump overcall.

With a seven-card suit, a weak jump overcall can be made at the three level, similar to a three-level preemptive opening bid. For example, consider South's call with this hand after East opens 1♠.

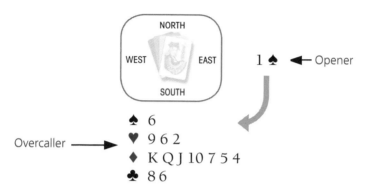

3♦. With a good seven-card suit, South would have opened 3♦ if East had passed. South can make the same call after East opens 1♠ but it is now a weak jump overcall instead of a preemptive three-level opening bid.

As with any preemptive bid, South should be more cautious when vulnerable since the potential penalty is larger. With only six playing tricks, South might prefer to pass with this hand when vulnerable. South shouldn't make a simple overcall of 2♦ since North would expect South to hold a stronger hand for a simple two-level overcall—about the values for an opening bid.

SUMMARY

Requirements for a Simple Overcall

Distribution: A good five-card suit or a six-card or longer suit.
Strength: 7 or more high-card points at the one level.
              13 or more points at the two level or higher.

Advancing an Overcall with Support

6–9 points: With 3-card support, raise to the cheapest level.
              With 4-card support, raise to the three level.
              With 5-card support, raise to the game level.
10+ points: Cuebid the opponents' suit, showing interest in
              reaching game.

Advancing in a New Suit

Distribution: A good five-card suit or a six-card longer suit.
Strength: 6 or more points at the one level;
              11 or more points at the two level.
              A new suit advance is not forcing[20].

Advancing in Notrump

6–10 points: Bid notrump at the cheapest level.
11–12 points: Jump in notrump.
13+ points: Cuebid then bid notrump.

Requirements for a 1NT Overcall

Distribution: Balanced hand.
Strength: 15–18 points (some strength in the opponent's suit).

Requirements for a Preemptive Jump Overcall

Distribution: A good six-card suit at the two level.
              A good seven-card suit at the three ievel.
Strength: A weak hand.

[20] Some partnerships prefer to treat a new suit response as forcing.

Quiz – Part I

Neither side is vulnerable. East opens 1♥. What call would South make with the following hands?

West	North	East	South
		1♥	?

a) ♠ A K J 8 5
   ♥ 7 4
   ♦ K J 6 2
   ♣ 8 3

b) ♠ 7 3
   ♥ K 4
   ♦ A Q 10 8 6 3
   ♣ A 9 6

c) ♠ A J 10 9 5
   ♥ 2
   ♦ 8 6 3
   ♣ K 10 9 4

d) ♠ A 4
   ♥ Q 9 3
   ♦ J 6 2
   ♣ Q 8 7 6 2

e) ♠ 9
   ♥ J 6
   ♦ A Q 10 8 4
   ♣ A Q J 7 3

f) ♠ 7 3
   ♥ A K J 10 8
   ♦ A J 5
   ♣ 8 7 5

g) ♠ A 8 3
   ♥ K Q 9
   ♦ Q 10 5
   ♣ A J 10 7

h) ♠ A K J 10 8 5
   ♥ 5
   ♦ 7 6 3
   ♣ 9 5 4

i) ♠ 10 8 3
   ♥ 9 6
   ♦ 5
   ♣ A Q J 10 7 4 3

East-West are vulnerable and North-South are non vulnerable. West opens 1♠, North passes, and East responds 2♦. What call would South make with the following hands?

West	North	East	South
1♠	Pass	2♦	?

j) ♠ K 8 3
   ♥ K J 10 8 5
   ♦ 7 4
   ♣ Q 9 5

k) ♠ 8 4
   ♥ A K Q 9 8
   ♦ 8 6
   ♣ K J 10 3

l) ♠ 5
   ♥ 9 7 3
   ♦ K 4
   ♣ A Q J 10 8 6 3

Answers to Quiz – Part I

a) 1♠. With a good five-card spade suit and 12 high-card points, make a simple overcall at the one level.

b) 2♦. With 13 high-card points and a good six-card diamond suit, this hand is strong enough for a simple overcall at the two level.

c) 1♠. Although there are only 8 high-card points, with a good five-card spade suit that's enough to make a simple overcall at the one level.

d) Pass. With 9 high-card points and a poor five-card suit which would have to be bid at the two level, this hand is unsuitable for an overcall.

e) 2♦. With 14 high-card points plus 1 length point for each five-card suit, there is enough strength to make a simple overcall at the two level. With two five-card suits, bid the higher-ranking.

f) Pass. East has a five-card or longer heart suit, so South doesn't want to compete in the same suit. South is happy to defend with hearts as the trump suit.

g) 1NT. With a balanced hand and 16 high-card points, South would have opened 1NT if East had passed. After East opens, South can overcall 1NT to describe the hand. South has some strength in hearts, the opponents' suit, in case that suit is led against a notrump contract.

h) 2♠ (1♠). Although South could overcall 1♠, a weak jump overcall to 2♠ is more descriptive. It shows a good six-card suit but a weak hand, similar to an opening weak two-bid.

i) 3♣. A jump overcall to the three level is also preemptive, similar to an opening bid at the three level. If South were to make a simple overcall of 2♣, North would expect a stronger hand.

j) Pass. South has a good five-card suit but not enough strength to make an overcall at the two level.

k) 2♥. With both East and West bidding, it's a little risky to come into the auction at the two level, but South has a good five-card suit and a good hand. South would certainly like North to lead a heart if East-West buy the contract.

l) 3♣. This time, South has to overcall at the three level. South has a good seven-card suit and North-South are non vulnerable, so it's not too risky.

Quiz – Part II

Both sides are vulnerable. West opens 1♦. North overcalls 1♥ and East passes. What call would South make, as advancer, with each of the following hands?

WEST	NORTH	EAST	SOUTH
1♦	1♥	PASS	?

a) ♠ J 9 7 4 3
   ♥ 4
   ♦ Q 8 2
   ♣ 10 7 6 3

b) ♠ 7 3
   ♥ J 9 4
   ♦ J 8 4
   ♣ A J 7 5 3

c) ♠ 5
   ♥ Q 10 8 5
   ♦ 8 6 5 3
   ♣ K 7 4 2

d) ♠ 10 8 7 4 2
   ♥ K 9 8 6 3
   ♦ 8 7 3
   ♣ —

e) ♠ K 10 4
   ♥ K J 6
   ♦ Q 10
   ♣ J 9 7 4 3

f) ♠ J 4
   ♥ A 10 8
   ♦ A 8 6 2
   ♣ K Q 7 5

g) ♠ A Q J 8 7
   ♥ 6 3
   ♦ 8 6 4
   ♣ K 9 2

h) ♠ Q 7 4 3
   ♥ 8 5
   ♦ A Q 10
   ♣ J 9 7 5

i) ♠ Q J 7
   ♥ K 4
   ♦ K Q 10 5
   ♣ 10 9 7 3

North-South are vulnerable and East-West are non vulnerable. East opens 1♣, South overcalls 1♠, and West passes. North advances to 2♠ and East passes. What rebid would South make, as the over-caller, with the following hands?

WEST	NORTH	EAST	SOUTH
		1♣	1♠
PASS	2♠	PASS	?

j) ♠ K Q 10 8 5
   ♥ 6 4 2
   ♦ A 7 5
   ♣ 6 4

k) ♠ K J 10 7 5 3
   ♥ Q 4
   ♦ K Q 7
   ♣ A 5

l) ♠ A J 8 7 6 3
   ♥ 4
   ♦ A K J
   ♣ K 8 4

Answers to Quiz – Part II

a)   Pass. South doesn't like North's choice of trump suit but, with only 3 high-card points and 1 length point, South doesn't have enough strength to bid another suit or notrump.

b)   2♥. With three-card support for hearts and 7 high-card points plus 1 dummy point for the doubleton spade, South has enough to raise partner's suit.

c)   3♥. South has 5 high-card points and 3 dummy points for the singleton. With a hand in the 6-9 point range and four-card support, South makes a preemptive raise to the three level.

d)   4♥. There are 3 high-card points and 5 dummy points for the void in clubs. With five-card heart support, South makes a preemptive raise to the game level. If North can't make 4♥, it's likely the opponents can make something.

e)   2♦. With support for partner and 10 high-card points plus 1 dummy point, South cuebids the opponents' suit. If North makes a minimum rebid of 2♥, South can pass. This avoids getting the partnership too high when North has a minimum one-level overcall.

f)   2♦. With support for partner's suit and 14 high-card points plus 1 dummy point for the doubleton spade, South starts with a 2♦ cuebid. If North makes a minimum rebid of 2♥, South can raise to 3♥ to invite partner to bid game.

g)   1♠. With no fit for hearts but a good five-card spade suit and 10 high-card points, South can advance in a new suit. This is not forcing.

h)   1NT. With 9 high-card points and strength in the opponents' suit, South has enough to advance to 1NT.

i)   2NT. With 11 high-card points and strength in diamonds, South makes an invitational jump to 2NT.

j)   Pass. With 9 high-card points plus 1 length point for the five-card suit, South doesn't have much extra for the overcall. North's raise shows about 6-9 points, so South settles for partscore.

k)   3♠. North has about 6-9 points and South has 15 high-card points plus 2 length points for the six-card suit. Game is possible if North has 8 or 9 points rather than 6 or 7. South invites North to continue to game by rebidding 3♠.

l)   4♠. South has 16 high-card points plus 2 length points for the six-card suit. Even if North has only 7 points, there should be enough combined strength to go for the game bonus.

Quiz – Part III

Neither side is vulnerable. East opens 1♦, South overcalls 1♠, West passes, North advances to 2♦, and East passes. What does South bid?

WEST	NORTH	EAST	SOUTH
		1♦	1♠
PASS	2♦	PASS	?

a) ♠ A J 10 8 5
   ♥ K 3
   ♦ 10 9 2
   ♣ J 7 3

b) ♠ A K J 10 7 3
   ♥ K Q 4
   ♦ 8 4
   ♣ 7 3

c) ♠ K J 10 7 5
   ♥ J 3
   ♦ 5
   ♣ A K J 7 5

Both sides are vulnerable. East opens 1♣, South overcalls 1♥, West passes, North advances to 1♠, and East passes. What is South's call?

WEST	NORTH	EAST	SOUTH
		1♣	1♥
PASS	1♠	PASS	?

d) ♠ 8 6
   ♥ Q J 10 8 5
   ♦ A J 4
   ♣ 8 6 2

e) ♠ K 8 4
   ♥ A Q 10 7 3
   ♦ K 4
   ♣ 10 6 2

f) ♠ 8
   ♥ A K 10 9 5
   ♦ A Q J 3
   ♣ 7 5 2

East-West are vulnerable, North-South are non vulnerable. West opens 1♥, North overcalls 1♠, East passes and South cuebids 2♥ as advancer. West passes and North rebids 2♠. What rebid would South make?

WEST	NORTH	EAST	SOUTH
1♥	1♠	PASS	2♥
PASS	2♠	PASS	?

g) ♠ A 9 5
   ♥ J 4 2
   ♦ K Q 7 5
   ♣ J 6 3

h) ♠ Q 10 6
   ♥ A 6 3 2
   ♦ K 7
   ♣ A J 6 5

i) ♠ A Q 7 5
   ♥ 7 3
   ♦ A K 5 4
   ♣ K J 4

Answers to Quiz – Part III

a) 2♠. North's 2♦ cuebid of the opponents' suit is forcing, showing 10 or more points. With nothing much extra for the overcall, South rebids spades at the cheapest level.

b) 3♠. With 13 high-card points plus 2 length points for the six-card suit, South has extra strength for the one-level overcall. South can show the extra strength and the extra length in spades suit by rebidding the suit with a jump.

c) 3♣. North's 2♦ cuebid is forcing. With a good hand for the overcall, South shows the second suit.

d) Pass. A new suit by advancer is not forcing. With nothing extra, South passes and stops in partscore. North should have a good five-card or longer spade suit. Since North didn't raise hearts, it's likely that North has fewer than three hearts.

e) 2♠. With more than a minimum for the overcall and support for North's spades, South raises to 2♠.

f) 2♦. South doesn't like North's spades but has a good hand for the overcall. South bids the second suit, giving North a choice of hearts or diamonds.

g) Pass. North has made a minimum rebid, showing nothing extra for the one-level overcall. Game is unlikely, so South settles for partscore.

h) 3♠. With 14 high-card points plus 1 dummy point for the doubleton diamond, South has enough to invite North to game even though North has promised nothing extra. If North has as much as 11 or 12 points, game should be reasonable. With less, North can pass.

i) 4♠. Even opposite a minimum one-level overcall, there should be enough combined strength for game since South has four-card support and 17 high-card points plus 1 dummy point for the doubleton heart. South didn't advance to 4♠ right away because that would show a weaker hand of about 6-9 points.

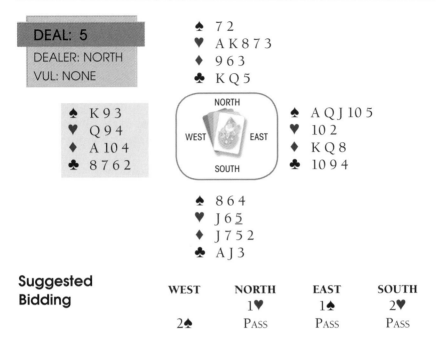

DEAL: 5

DEALER: NORTH

VUL: NONE

NORTH

♠ 7 2
♥ A K 8 7 3
♦ 9 6 3
♣ K Q 5

WEST

♠ K 9 3
♥ Q 9 4
♦ A 10 4
♣ 8 7 6 2

EAST

♠ A Q J 10 5
♥ 10 2
♦ K Q 8
♣ 10 9 4

SOUTH

♠ 8 6 4
♥ J 6 5
♦ J 7 5 2
♣ A J 3

Suggested Bidding

WEST	NORTH	EAST	SOUTH
	1♥	1♠	2♥
2♠	Pass	Pass	Pass

North has 12 high-card points plus 1 length point for the five-card suit, enough to open the bidding. North opens 1♥.

East has 12 high-card points plus 1 length point for the five-card suit. If North had passed, East would open 1♠. After North's opening bid, East can compete for the contract by overcalling 1♠.

South, the responder, has three-card support for North's major suit and 7 high-card points. That's enough to raise to 2♥.

West, the advancer, has 9 high-card points and three-card support for East's suit. West can continue the partnership's competition for the contract by raising to 2♠.

North has already described the hand by opening the bidding and passes with nothing extra to show.

Since West's raise is limited to about 9 points, East knows the partnership only has enough combined strength for partscore. East passes.

South has nothing extra to show and also passes. The contract is 2♠ with East as the declarer.

Suggested Opening Lead

South, on declarer's left, makes the opening lead. With no touching high cards in partner's suit, South leads low, the ♥5.

Declarer's Plan

After South makes the opening lead and the West hand comes down as the dummy, East makes a plan. As declarer, East's goal is to take at least 8 tricks to make the 2♠ contract. East begins by counting the sure winners: five sure tricks in spades and three in diamonds. That's a total of eight, exactly what is required.

> ┌── DECLARER'S PLAN—THE ABC'S ──┐
>
> Declarer: East   Contract: 2♠
>
> **ASSESS THE SITUATION**
> Goal   8
> Sure Tricks   8
> Extra Tricks Needed 0
>
> **BROWSE DECLARER'S CHECKLIST**
> Not applicable
>
> **CONSIDER THE ORDER**
> • Draw trumps.
> • Take the tricks and run.

With enough tricks to make the contract, declarer's priority is to draw trumps after gaining the lead. Suppose North wins the first two tricks with the ♥A-K and the defenders then take three club tricks. Whatever the defenders lead next, declarer can win. East can then start taking spade winners until the defenders have no trumps remaining. This takes three rounds because the five missing trumps are divided 3-2.

Once the opponents' trumps are drawn, it is safe to take three diamond winners. On the actual deal, East could have taken the diamond winners before drawing trumps, but that would not have worked if either opponent had a singleton or doubleton diamond.

Comments

If East-West did not compete for the contract, North-South would play the contract in 2♥. By using the overcall to compete, East-West will either be left to play in the makeable 2♠ contract or push North-South to 3♥, which can be defeated two tricks.

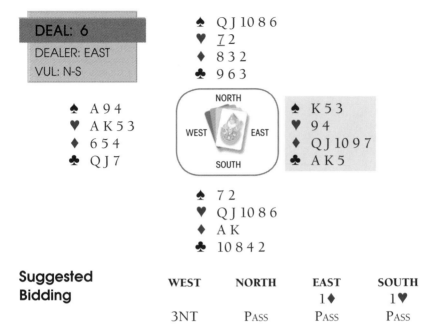

	NORTH	
	♠ Q J 10 8 6	
	♥ 7 2	
	♦ 8 3 2	
	♣ 9 6 3	

DEAL: 6
DEALER: EAST
VUL: N-S

WEST	EAST
♠ A 9 4	♠ K 5 3
♥ A K 5 3	♥ 9 4
♦ 6 5 4	♦ Q J 10 9 7
♣ Q J 7	♣ A K 5

SOUTH
♠ 7 2
♥ Q J 10 8 6
♦ A K
♣ 10 8 4 2

Suggested Bidding

WEST	NORTH	EAST	SOUTH
		1♦	1♥
3NT	Pass	Pass	Pass

East has 13 high-card points plus 1 point for the five-card diamond suit. East opens in the minor suit, 1♦.

South has only 10 high-card points plus 1 length point for the five-card suit but, with a good five-card heart suit and three of the top five honors, South can overcall at the one level.

West, the responder, has a balanced hand with 14 high-card points. Since East has opened the bidding, West decides How High, game, knowing the partnership has at least 27 combined points. With strength in hearts, the opponents' suit, West decides Where, notrump. West jumps to 3NT.

North, East, and South all pass, and the contract is 3NT played by West.

Suggested Opening Lead

North is on lead against 3NT. Without any information from the auction, North would lead the ♠Q, top of the solid sequence. After South's overcall, however, North leads the ♥7, top of the doubleton in partner's suit.

Declarer's Plan

West's goal is to take at least nine tricks to make the 3NT contract. West begins by counting the sure winners: two spades, two hearts, and three clubs for a total of seven tricks. Two more tricks are required.

West browses Declarer's Checklist. Declarer can plan to promote three extra winners in the diamond suit by driving out the ◆A and ◆K.

DECLARER'S PLAN—THE ABC'S
Declarer: West Contract: 3NT
ASSESS THE SITUATION
Goal 9
Sure Tricks 7
Extra Tricks Needed 2
BROWSE DECLARER'S CHECKLIST
Promotion: 3 in diamonds
Length
The Finesse
CONSIDER THE ORDER
• Develop the extra diamond tricks early.

After winning the ♥K, West leads to one of dummy's high diamonds to drive out the ◆K. South wins and leads another heart, driving out West's ♥A. Declarer can lead another high diamond to drive out the ◆A and establish dummy's remaining diamonds as winners.

Unfortunately for East-West, South can take enough heart winners to defeat the contract after winning the ◆A. North-South win the race to promote winners in their long suit, thanks to North's opening lead of the ♥7, partner's suit.

Comments

If North had led the ♠Q instead of a heart, declarer could make the contract. Declarer wins either the ♠A or ♠K and plays a high diamond to drive out the ◆K. South can lead another spade to drive out declarer's remaining high spade and establish North's remaining spades as winners. When declarer leads another high diamond, however, South wins the ◆A and has no spades to lead. Whatever South leads, declarer wins and takes the established diamond winners to make the contract with an *overtrick*.

The overcall is effective in getting the partnership off to the best opening lead and did not involve much risk. If East-West chose to defend against 1♥, that contract can only be defeated one trick, for a small penalty. If East-West choose to play in a partscore contract in diamonds, South's overcall has kept them from getting to 3NT.

DEAL: 7		♠ A Q 10 9 7
DEALER: SOUTH		♥ 8 6 3
VUL: E-W		♦ K Q J
		♣ 8 5

♠ 5	NORTH	♠ 4 2
♥ A K J 7 5 2	WEST EAST	♥ Q 10 4
♦ A 10 5		♦ 9 7 6 4 3
♣ A J 3	SOUTH	♣ K Q 7

♠ K J 8 6 3
♥ 9
♦ 8 2
♣ 10 9 6 4 2

Suggested Bidding

WEST	NORTH	EAST	SOUTH
			Pass
1♥	1♠	2♥	4♠
Pass(?)	Pass	Pass	

South passes. West opens 1♥ with 17 high-card points plus 2 length points for the six-card suit.

North, with a good five-card suit and 12 high-card points, over-calls 1♠.

East has three-card support for partner's hearts and 7 high-card points plus 1 dummy point for the doubleton spade. That's enough to raise to 2♥.

South has only 4 high-card points but can add 3 dummy points for the singleton heart and 1 dummy point for the doubleton diamond. With five-card support for partner's overcalled suit and a hand in the 6-9 point range, South can make a preemptive raise to the four level, 4♠. This is a two-way bid. With the good distributional hand, it is likely the partnership can take a lot of tricks with spades as the trump suit. At the same time, the jump to 4♠ makes it difficult for East-West to find their best spot.

West has a challenging decision over North's 4♠ advance. West

planned to bid 4♥ but would now have to bid 5♥ to win the contract. That may be too high. West might prefer to defend, hoping to defeat 4♠[21].

If West doesn't bid, North will become declarer in a 4♠ contract.

Suggested Opening Lead

East leads the ♥4, low from three or more cards with no touching honors in partner's suit.

Declarer's Plan

North's goal is to take at least ten tricks with spades as trumps. North counts five sure tricks in spades, but that's all. Five more tricks need to be developed.

North browses Declarer's Checklist. Two hearts can be trumped in dummy. Also, two tricks can be promoted in diamonds. That's not enough to make the contract, but it's the best declarer can do.

After West wins the first heart, the defenders may simply take their diamond and club

DECLARER'S PLAN—THE ABC'S		
Declarer: North	Contract: 4♠	
ASSESS THE SITUATION		
Goal	10	
Sure Tricks	5	
Extra Tricks Needed	5	
BROWSE DECLARER'S CHECKLIST		
Promotion:	2 in diamonds	
Length	0	
The Finesse	0	
Trumping in Dummy	2 in hearts	
CONSIDER THE ORDER		
• Draw trumps.		
• Develop the extra diamond tricks early.		
• Keep two trumps in dummy to ruff hearts.		

winners. If not, North can draw trumps on gaining the lead, promote the diamond winners and ruff two hearts with dummy's spades.

Comments

Although North-South can't make 4♠, going down one trick is a good result. East-West can make 4♥. They have six heart tricks, a diamond trick, and three club tricks. The penalty for being defeated in 4♠ is less than the score value for 4♥.

There is little East-West can do. If they bid 5♥, they will be defeated one trick. South's preemptive jump raise is effective.

---

[21] West might make a penalty double of 4♠ to increase the score for defeating the contract.

DEAL: 8
DEALER: WEST
VUL: BOTH

♠ A K 10 8 6
♥ Q 5 3
♦ A 10 7
♣ 10 6

♠ 4 2
♥ 10 8 4
♦ K Q J 6 2
♣ A K 4

NORTH
WEST EAST
SOUTH

♠ J 9 7 5
♥ 9
♦ 9 3
♣ J 9 7 5 3 2

♠ Q 3
♥ A K J 7 6 2
♦ 8 5 4
♣ Q 8

Suggested Bidding

WEST	NORTH	EAST	SOUTH
1♦	1♠	PASS	2♥
PASS	3♥	PASS	4♥
PASS	PASS	PASS	

West has 13 high-card points plus 1 length point for the five-card diamond suit. Although the hand is balanced, it isn't strong enough to open 1NT. West opens 1♦, the long suit.

North has 13 high-card points plus 1 point for the five-card spade suit, for a total of 14. With a good five-card suit, North overcalls 1♠.

East, with only 2 high-card points plus 2 length points for the six-card suit, doesn't have enough to respond and passes.

South doesn't have three-card support for North's spades but does have 12 high-card points plus 2 length points for the six-card heart suit. That's enough to advance in a new suit at the two level. The 2♥ bid is forward going, but not forcing. North can pass with a minimum overcall.

West doesn't have enough to bid again and passes.

North has three-card support for South's hearts and more than a minimum for the overcall. North raises to 3♥ to show the support and interest in reaching game.

After East passes, South has enough to continue to game with the knowledge that the partnership has a fit in hearts and North has more than the minimum strength for an overcall. South's 4♥ bid is followed by three passes, ending the auction.

Suggested Opening Lead

West could lead the ♦K, top of the solid sequence, or the ♣A, top of the touching honors in that suit, against South's 4♥ contract.

Declarer's Plan

South is declarer and the goal is to take ten tricks with hearts as trumps. South counts three sure tricks in spades, six in hearts, and one in diamonds. That's a total of ten tricks, exactly what is required.

West may take the first two club tricks and then lead the ♦K, or lead the ♦K initially. In either case, after winning the ♦A, declarer's priority is to draw trumps since there are enough tricks to make the contract. It will then be safe to take the spade winners.

> **DECLARER'S PLAN—THE ABC'S**
>
> Declarer: South   Contract: 4♥
>
> **ASSESS THE SITUATION**
> | | |
> |---|---|
> | Goal | 10 |
> | Sure Tricks | 10 |
> | Extra Tricks Needed | 0 |
>
> **BROWSE DECLARER'S CHECKLIST**
> Not applicable
>
> **CONSIDER THE ORDER**
> - Draw trumps first.
> - High card from the short side first in spades.

Since the spade suit is unevenly divided between the two hands, declarer starts with the ♠Q, high card from the short side first. The ♠2 is then played to dummy's ♠A and ♠K and declarer has ten tricks. On the third round of spades, declarer *discards* a diamond from the South hand.

Comments

If declarer tries to take the spade tricks before drawing trumps, West will trump the third round of spades. West can then take a diamond winner to go with the two club tricks to defeat the contract.

When you have a tough bidding decision, strive to be flexible. When you would like to be flexible, consider making a takeout double. When you double, you allow partner to assist in the decision-making process. When *you* do not know what to do, perhaps your *partner* will.

—Marty Bergen, Points Schmoints! (1995)

Takeout Doubles and Advances

The word double was introduced to bridge vocabulary in the last century. It was a way for the defenders to increase their score when they were reasonably sure the opponents had bid too much and could not make their contract. Since declarer's side would then lose a larger penalty for being defeated, this was referred to as a penalty double.

The use of the double expanded as the game evolved. When the auction is at a low level, there are few deals where you can be confident that the opponents can't make their contract, so a penalty double is usually premature. After all, declarer has to take only seven tricks at the one level in the partnership's chosen trump suit. Instead, the double can be put to more effective use.

The Classic Takeout Double

East opens the bidding 1♦ and it's South call.

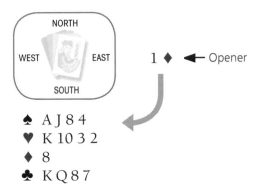

NORTH

WEST   EAST   1 ♦ ◄── Opener

SOUTH

♠ A J 8 4
♥ K 10 3 2
♦ 8
♣ K Q 8 7

With 13 high-card points, South would have opened if East had passed. That's no longer an option, but South would still like to compete for the privilege of naming the trump suit, preferring any trump suit other than diamonds. Yet the hand doesn't meet the requirements for an overcall; it has no five-card or longer suit.

The double can be used to solve this dilemma. Since you would rarely want to double the opponents for penalty at the one level in a trump suit of their choosing, the double is assigned another meaning. It is used to ask partner to choose a trump suit. Basically, the double sends the message, "I have enough strength to compete for the contract; I'd like you to choose the trump suit." Used in this manner, the double is referred to as a *takeout double*. Partner is being asked to take the double out into one of the *unbid* suits, a suit that hasn't been bid by the opponents.

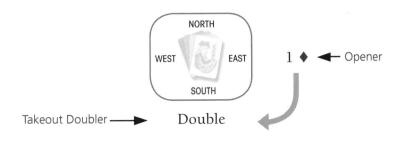

NORTH

WEST   EAST   1 ♦ ◄── Opener

SOUTH

Takeout Doubler ──► Double

Guidelines for a Takeout Double

The takeout double shows support for whichever suit partner chooses. After all, you're asking partner to pick a suit. You don't want to play in a contract where the opponents have more trumps than your side. It would be nice if you could always have at least four cards in whichever suit partner chooses. In practice, you may have three-card support for one of the possible suits, but you don't want to stray too much further from the ideal unless you have extra strength.

The takeout double requires the same values needed to open the bidding, about 13 or more valuation points. The high-card valuation points are the same as those used for opening the bidding or responding: Ace – 4; King – 3; Queen – 2; Jack – 1. If you ask partner to pick the suit and your side wins the auction, your hand will go down on the table as the dummy. For this reason, value the distribution using dummy points instead of length points: void – 5; singleton – 3; doubleton – 1.

The Takeout Double

- Support for the unbid suits:
    At least three-card support,
    preferably four-card support
- 13 or more total points, counting high-card points and dummy points:
    void = 5;
    singleton = 3;
    doubleton = 1.

Examples

The following hands meet the requirements for a takeout double by South after East opens 1♦.

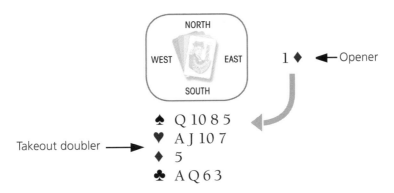

Takeout doubler ⟶
♠ Q 10 8 5
♥ A J 10 7
♦ 5
♣ A Q 6 3

Double. This is the ideal *pattern* for a takeout double, shortness in diamonds, the opponent's suit, and four-card support for each of the unbid suits. South has 13 high-card points and can add 3 dummy points for the singleton diamond.

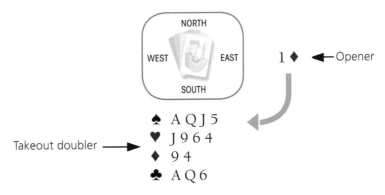

Takeout doubler ⟶
♠ A Q J 5
♥ J 9 6 4
♦ 9 4
♣ A Q 6

Double. This hand qualifies for a takeout double because of the four-card support for hearts and spades and reasonable three-card support if partner chooses clubs. South has 14 high-card points plus 1 dummy point for the doubleton diamond.

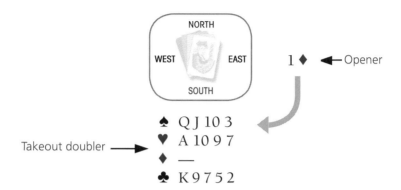

♠ Q J 10 3
♥ A 10 9 7
♦ —
♣ K 9 7 5 2

Takeout doubler ⟶

Double. 10 high-card points plus 5 dummy points for the diamond void meets the requirements for a takeout double. With a five-card suit, South might consider making an overcall. However, clubs would have to be bid at the two level and the suit is not very good and the hand is not strong enough. The takeout double is more descriptive and gives the partnership the best chance of finding a suitable trump fit.

The following hands don't meet the requirements for a takeout double by South after East opens 1♦.

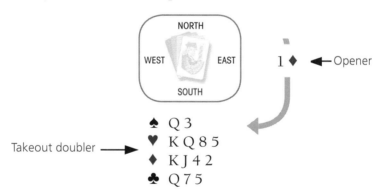

♠ Q 3
♥ K Q 8 5
♦ K J 4 2
♣ Q 7 5

Takeout doubler ⟶

Pass. This hand isn't suitable for an overcall (no five-card suit) or a takeout double of 1♦. Although South has support for hearts, there isn't support if North chooses spades, and the support isn't that good if North picks clubs.

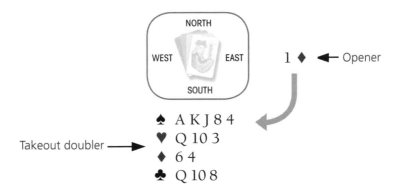

1♠. On this hand, South has a definite preference for spades and overcalls 1♠. South doesn't want to make a takeout double asking North to choose the suit when spades is the suit South would like

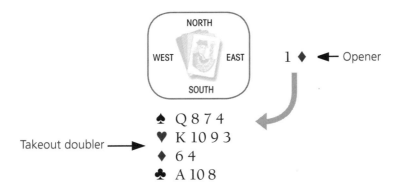

to suggest as trumps.

Pass. South has support for the unbid suits but not enough strength to make a takeout double—9 high-card points plus 1 dummy point for the doubleton diamond. North would expect a better hand.

The Takeout Double After Both Opponents Have Bid

The takeout double can be used after both opponents have bid[22]. You are still asking partner to pick a trump suit other than the suit(s) suggested by the opponents. For example, suppose the opponent on your left opens 1♣, partner passes, and the opponent on your right responds 1♥:

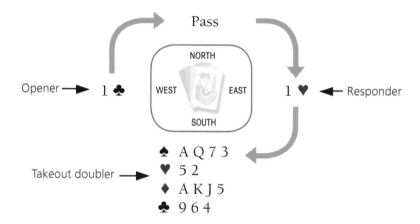

Double. In this auction, there are only two unbid suits, spades and diamonds. South has support for both suits and 14 high-card points plus 1 dummy point for the doubleton heart. By making a takeout double, South is asking North to choose either spades or diamonds as a trump suit.

---

[22] See Practice Deal #32 for an example of a takeout double after both opponents have bid.

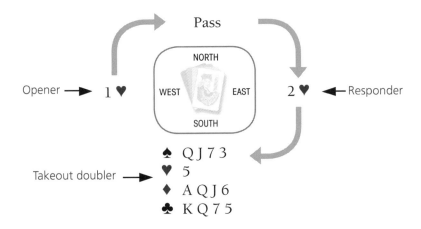

Pass

Opener → 1 ♥   WEST   NORTH   EAST   2 ♥ ← Responder
                        SOUTH

Takeout doubler →   ♠ Q J 7 3
                    ♥ 5
                    ♦ A Q J 6
                    ♣ K Q 7 5

Double. After East raises West's suit, there are still three unbid suits and South has support for all of them. By doubling, the partnership is committed to at least the two level if North chooses spades, or the three level if North chooses a minor suit, either clubs or diamonds. With 15 high-card points plus 3 dummy points for the singleton heart, South has enough strength to get into the auction.

In general, the higher the level at which the takeout double is made, the more strength the doubler requires since the partnership will be committed to taking more tricks[23].

---

[23] See Practice Deals #17 and #29 for examples of takeout doubles at higher levels.

Advancing a Takeout Double

The partner of the opening bidder is referred to as the responder. The partner of a player making an overcall or a takeout double is referred to as the advancer.

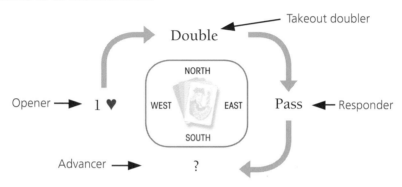

Guidelines for Advancing a Takeout Double

By now, you may not be surprised to hear that the requirements for advancing a takeout double are not the same as those for responding to an opening bid or for advancing an overcall. There's a reason for the differences.

First of all, when partner opens the bidding or makes an overcall, partner is suggesting a trump suit and you are invited to pass or to bid again. When partner makes a takeout double, you're being asked to pick the trump suit. This is more than a request; it's a demand, a forcing bid.

Choosing the Level

Since you're not expected to pass, you must bid, even with no points! There will also be times when you want to bid and explore getting to a game contract. Or, you may have the values to bid a game bonus level opposite your partner's takeout double. The guidelines take this into consideration:

Advancing a Takeout Double

- 0–8 points   Bid at the cheapest level.
- 9–11 points   Make an invitational bid by
  jumping one level[24].
- 12+ points   Get the partnership to game.

Choosing the Suit

Partner has asked you to choose a trump suit and you generally pick your longest suit, since that should be the longest combined suit for the partnership. With a choice between a major suit and a minor suit, the major suit is preferable. Major suit contracts are worth more and fewer tricks are required if you are going for a game bonus. As a guideline, with a choice of suits, bid the higher-ranking.

Examples with 0-8 points

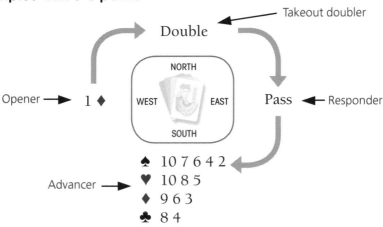

1♠. North asked South to choose a suit and has made a forcing bid. If South passes, West will be left to play in a contract of 1♦ doubled. Diamonds is the opponents' choice of trump suit, North

---

[24] Depending on the level of the takeout double and responder's actions, there may not always be room for advancer to jump. This is discussed further in Chapter 4.

is unlikely to have more than one or two diamonds, and it's only the one level, so declarer is likely to make the contract, probably with overtricks. North is aware South could have no high cards and is merely asking South to give an opinion on the best trump suit for the partnership.

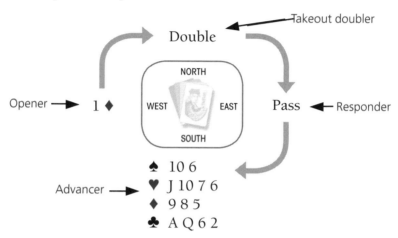

1♥. Although South's clubs are stronger than the hearts, it's better to show the major suit. South can do so at a lower level and major suit contracts are worth more than minor suits. With two suits of equal length, choose the major suit. With 0–8 points, South bids at the cheapest level.

Sometimes, the cheapest level available is the two level or higher:

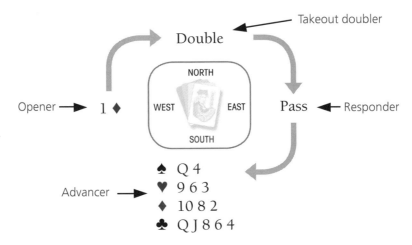

2♣. South bids the longest suit at the cheapest level. Although South is bidding a new suit at the two level, 11 or more points are not needed when advancing a takeout double. Also 2♣ is not forcing. North asked South to bid and the situation is more comparable to raising North's suit than introducing a new suit.

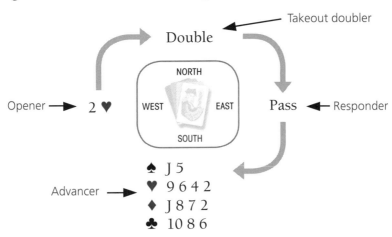

3♦. When North makes a takeout double of West's 2♥ opening bid, the cheapest level available to bid the longest suit is the three level. South isn't promising any strength by advancing to 3♦. North will have taken this possibility into account when choosing to make a takeout double at this level and should have extra strength.

Examples with 9–11 points

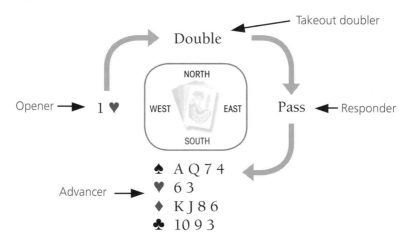

Double — Takeout doubler

Opener → 1 ♥

Pass ← Responder

NORTH
WEST EAST
SOUTH

Advancer →
♠ A Q 7 4
♥ 6 3
♦ K J 8 6
♣ 10 9 3

2♠. South would advance to 1♠ with a hand in the 0–8 point range. Here there are 10 high-card points and the partnership is close to the combined strength needed for a game bonus. By jumping a level of the bidding when advancing partner's takeout double, South sends an invitational message. North can pass with the minimum values for a takeout double or bid on to game with a little extra.

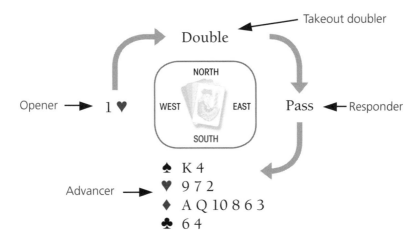

Takeout doubler

Double

NORTH

Opener → 1 ♥   WEST   EAST   Pass ← Responder

SOUTH

♠ K 4
Advancer → ♥ 9 7 2
♦ A Q 10 8 6 3
♣ 6 4

3♦. With 9 high-card points plus 2 length points for the six-card suit, South makes an invitational bid by jumping a level, advancing to 3♦ rather than 2♦. The partnership should be safe at the three level since North is showing an opening bid with support for the suit South chooses. If North has extra strength, a game contract is in sight.

Examples with 12+ points

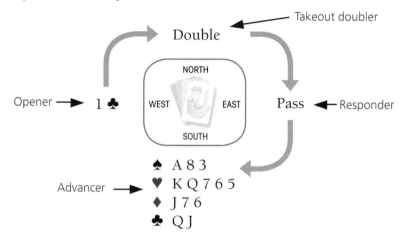

4♥. South has 13 high-card points plus 1 length point for the five-card heart suit. South bids to a contract the partnership should be able to make. North has the values for an opening bid with support for hearts. That's enough information to tell South what to do. South knows How High, game; South knows Where, hearts.

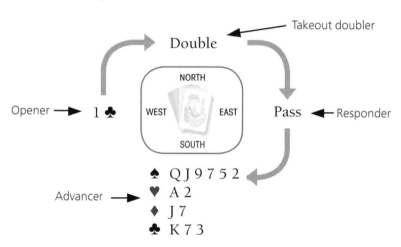

4♠. South has 11 high-card points plus 2 length points for the six-card suit. Game in spades looks like the best spot for the partnership.

When Advancer Doesn't Have to Bid

Advancer is expected to bid, even with no points, if the next player passes after the takeout double. Otherwise, the opponents would be left to play in their doubled contract. If advancer's right-hand opponent bids, however, advancer can pass with a weak hand:

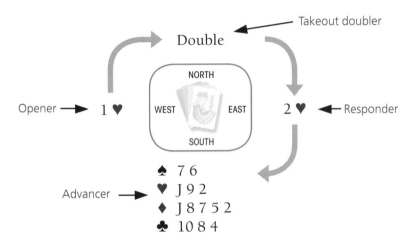

Pass. If East had passed, South would bid 2♦ to prevent the opponents from playing in 1♥ doubled. When East raises opener's heart suit to 2♥, South is no longer obliged to bid.

Although South doesn't have to bid, South may want to compete after East bids. North's takeout double has promised 13 or more points and shown a desire to compete for the contract. So, with 6 or more points, South should try to bid when possible. For example:

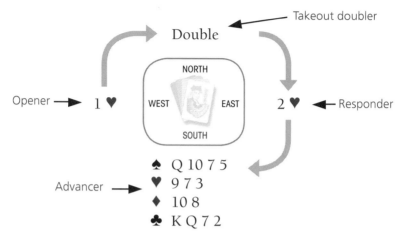

2♠. South is no longer forced to bid after East's raise to 2♥ but, with 7 high-card points, South should compete for the contract. North-South likely have as much combined strength as East-West, so they don't want to let East-West choose the trump suit without a struggle. 2♠ is not a jump, so North won't expect any more than 6–8 points.

Advancing in Notrump

The takeout doubler has asked advancer to choose an unbid suit as a trump suit. Advancer seldom considers playing in notrump, especially since the takeout doubler is usually short in the opponents' suit. With length and strength in the opponents' suit, however, advancer can consider bidding notrump, using this guideline[25]:

Advancing in Notrump

With strength in the opponents' suit and no better option, bid notrump using the following ranges:

- 6–10 points   Bid notrump at the cheapest level.
- 11–12 points   Bid notrump, jumping a level.
- 13+ points   Bid game in notrump.

---

[25] With 0–5 points, don't bid notrump. Pick an unbid suit, even if it is only three cards.

Here are examples for South after West opens 1♦, North doubles, and East passes.

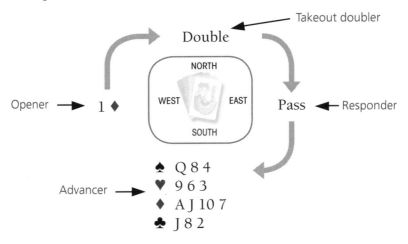

1NT. With length and strength in diamonds, the opponents' suit, and 8 high-card points, an advance of 1NT is the best option for South.

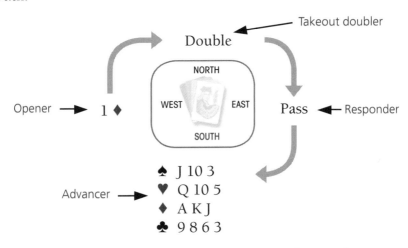

2NT. With 11 high-card points, South has enough to make a jump response to 3♣. With so much strength in diamonds, however, an advance of 2NT is a better description of the hand.

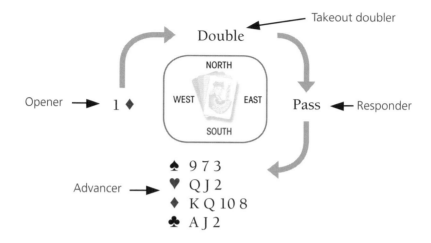

3NT. With 13 high-card points opposite North's takeout double, the partnership belongs in a game contract. With enough length and strength in diamonds, South chooses 3NT.

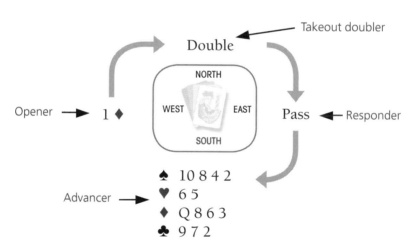

1♠. Although South's best suit is diamonds, there isn't enough strength to bid 1NT. South simply bids spades at the cheapest level.

Advancer's Forcing Bid

The bid of a new suit by advancer is not forcing and shows 0–8 points. Even a jump by advancer is not forcing, showing an invitational hand of about 9-11 points. With 12 or more points, advancer can jump to a game contract but advancer sometimes needs more information from the takeout doubler to help decide WHERE the partnership belongs. The only forcing bid available to advancer is the cuebid, the bid of the opponents' suit[26].

For example, suppose West opens 1♦, North doubles, and East passes:

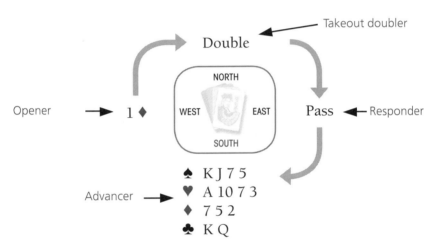

With 13 high-card points opposite North's takeout double, South knows the partnership has enough combined strength for game, but which game? South could guess to jump to 4♥ or 4♠, but the partnership might land in a 4-3 trump fit. Ideally, North will have four-card support for whichever suit South chooses, but North will sometimes have only three-card support.

The solution is to make a forcing call, 2♦, a cuebid of the opponents' suit. Diamonds is the one suit North and South do not

---

[26] See Practice Deal #31 for an example of using the cuebid to reach the best contract.

want to choose as trumps. After the cuebid of 2♦, North can make a descriptive bid. With a four-card or longer heart suit[27], North bids 2♥. South now jumps to 4♥, assured that the partnership will be in an eight-card fit. With only three hearts, North can bid 2♠ with a four-card suit. South now jumps to 4♠, again assured of landing in the partnership's best fit.

Rebids by the Takeout Doubler

The takeout double promises at least 13 points but could be made on a much stronger hand. The takeout doubler's strength will fall into one of three ranges:

Doubler's Strength Categories	
Minimum	13–16 points
Medium	17–18 points
Maximum	19+ points

Advancer's bid will also fall into one of three ranges:

Advancer's Strength Categories	
Minimum (a bid at the cheapest level)	0–8 points
Medium (an invitational jump)	9–11 points
Maximum (a jump to game or cuebid)	12+ points

After making a takeout double, combine these two pieces of information to decide whether you should bid again.

---

[27] With four hearts and four spades, North bids hearts, bidding "up the line."

Rebid by Doubler When Advancer Shows a Minimum Hand (0–8)

When advancer bids at the cheapest level, the doubler must be cautious. Advancer was forced to bid and may have no points. With a minimum takeout double, pass; with a medium hand, raise one level; with a maximum, make a jump raise[28].

In the following examples, South opens 1♦ and West makes a takeout double. North passes and East advances 1♥. South, the opener, passes and West, the doubler, now has to decide on a rebid.

West	North	East	South
			1♦
Double	Pass	1♥	Pass
?			

NORTH
WEST   EAST
SOUTH

♠ K 10 8 3
♥ A Q 7 5
♦ 7 4
♣ K J 6

Pass. West has 13 high-card points plus 1 dummy point for the doubleton diamond. East has at most 8 points and could have much less. The partnership is high enough.

♠ A Q 7 5
♥ K Q 9 2
♦ 7
♣ K J 8 2

2♥. West has 15 high-card points plus 3 dummy points for the singleton diamond—putting this hand in the medium strength category. East could have 7 or 8 points, so West makes a mild invitation by raising one level. West doesn't bid any higher in case East has a very weak hand.

♠ K Q J 5
♥ A J 7 2
♦ 9 3
♣ A K J

3♥. West has 19 high-card points plus 1 dummy point for the singleton diamond. Even though West is in the maximum range for a takeout double, West can't afford to take the partnership to game. East may have zero points. Instead, West issues a strong invitation by making a jump raise. East can bid game with 5 or 6 points or more, but can still stop in partscore with a very weak hand.

---

[28] See Practice Deal #21 for an example of doubler's rebid with a maximum strength hand.

Rebid by Doubler When Advancer Shows a Medium Hand (9–11)

If advancer makes an invitational bid by jumping a level, accept the invitation with about 15 or more points. With a bare minimum of 13 or 14 points, pass and stop in partscore.

West	North	East	South	
			1♦	NORTH
Double	Pass	2♥	Pass	WEST · EAST
?				SOUTH

♠ A J 6 2
♥ Q 9 3
♦ 6 5
♣ K Q 9 4

Pass. West has 12 high-card points plus 1 dummy point for the doubleton diamond, a bare minimum. Even if East has 11 points, the partnership does not have the combined strength for game.

♠ K Q 7 3
♥ K J 7 5
♦ 6
♣ A J 5 2

4♥. With 14 high-card points plus 3 dummy point for the singleton diamond, West has more than enough to accept East's invitational bid.

Rebid by Doubler When Advancer Shows a Maximium Hand (12+)

With 12 or more points, advancer will usually have chosen a game contract, so you won't have to bid again unless you are interested in reaching a slam contract. If advancer has made a cuebid, however, you must bid again, making a further description of the hand.

West	North	East	South	
			1♦	NORTH
Double	Pass	2♦	Pass	WEST · EAST
?				SOUTH

♠ K Q 8 3
♥ A 7 5
♦ 9 8
♣ A 10 9 5

2♠. Advancer's cuebid asks for help in deciding where to play the contract. With a four-card spade suit but only a three-card heart suit, 2♠ is the most descriptive call.

The Double to Show a Strong Overcall

The double is a very flexible bid since it takes up no room on the Bidding Ladder. Consider this hand for South after East opens 1♣.

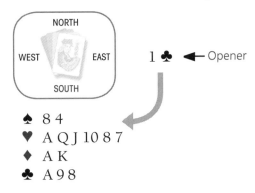

	NORTH		
WEST		EAST	1 ♣ ◀— Opener
	SOUTH		

♠ 8 4
♥ A Q J 10 8 7
♦ A K
♣ A 9 8

South doesn't have three-card support for either diamonds or spades and, with an excellent six-card heart suit, the hand appears more suitable for an overcall than a takeout double. With 18 high-card points plus 2 length points for the six-card suit, the hand is too strong for an overcall of 1♥. A simple overcall at the one level shows about 7-17 points, so North would not expect such a strong hand. Also, a jump to 2♥ would be preemptive, showing a weak hand, not a strong hand.

To show a hand too strong to overcall, start with a double—a forcing bid. North will assume this is a takeout double and bid one of the unbid suits, 1♠ for example. At the next opportunity, South bids hearts. This shows a hand too strong for an overcall[29]. North can still pass, but is now aware than South holds about 18 or more points. North doesn't need much to move toward a game contract.

Here is another example after East opens 1♠.

---

[29] With an even stronger hand, South doubles first and then jumps in the long suit at the next opportunity or cuebids the opponents' suit.

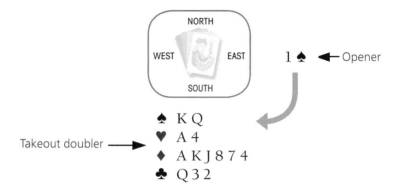

NORTH

WEST　　EAST　　　　1 ♠　← Opener

SOUTH

♠ K Q
Takeout doubler ——→ ♥ A 4
♦ A K J 8 7 4
♣ Q 3 2

Double. With 19 high-card points, South is too strong to overcall 2♦. Instead, South starts with a double. If North bids 2♥, for example, South will next bid 3♦, showing a very strong hand[30].

---

[30] See Practice Deal #25 for an example of using a takeout double to show a strong hand.

SUMMARY

Requirements for a Takeout Double

- Distribution: Support for the unbid suits.
  - at least three-card support, preferably four-card support
- Strength: 13 or more points, counting dummy points.
  - void – 5; singleton – 3; doubleton – 1

Advancing a Takeout Double

- 0–8 points: Bid at the cheapest level.
- 9–11 points: Make an invitational bid by jumping a level.
- 12+ points: Get the partnership to game.

Advancing in Notrump

With strength in the opponents' suit and no better option, bid notrump using the following ranges:

- 6 – 10 points: Bid notrump at the cheapest level.
- 11-12 points: Bid notrump, jumping a level.
- 13+ points: Bid game in notrump

Advancer's Forcing Bid

When advancer needs more information to decide How High and Where to play, a cuebid of the opponents' suit is forcing.

Rebids by the Takeout Doubler

The takeout doubler's strength falls approximately into these ranges:

- Minimum: 13–16 points.
- Medium: 17–18 points.
- Maximum: 19+ points.

The takeout doubler combines this with the approximate strength shown by advancer to decide whether to bid again.

Quiz – Part I

Neither side is vulnerable. East opens the bidding 1♥. What call would South make with the following hands?

West	North	East	South
		1♥	?

a) ♠ K 10 7 5
   ♥ 7
   ♦ A J 6 2
   ♣ A 9 8 3

b) ♠ A Q J 10 4
   ♥ 4 2
   ♦ K 8 4
   ♣ K 9 7

c) ♠ Q 10 9 7
   ♥ —
   ♦ A 10 8 3
   ♣ K J 8 6 2

d) ♠ Q 8 7
   ♥ 5 3
   ♦ A 9 6 2
   ♣ K 10 7 6

e) ♠ A 10 8 3
   ♥ 9 4
   ♦ Q 9 5
   ♣ A Q 7 4

f) ♠ 9
   ♥ A 9 5 3
   ♦ A J 6 2
   ♣ K J 7 6

Both sides are vulnerable. West opens the bidding 1♦. North passes and East responds 1♠. What call would South make with each of the following hands?

West	North	East	South
1♦	Pass	1♠	?

g) ♠ 4 3
   ♥ A Q 7 5
   ♦ 10 8 2
   ♣ A K J 3

h) ♠ Q 5
   ♥ Q J 5
   ♦ K 5 3 2
   ♣ K J 4 2

i) ♠ 3
   ♥ Q J 9 7 4
   ♦ A 4
   ♣ A 10 7 5 3

Answers to Quiz – Part I

a) Double. With support for the unbid suits and 12 high-card points plus 3 dummy points for the singleton heart, South makes a takeout double.

b) 1♠. South has the strength and support for a takeout double but, with a clear preference for spades as the trump suit, an overcall of 1♠ is a more descriptive way to enter the auction.

c) Double. Although there are only 10 high-card points, South can add 5 dummy points for the void when considering a takeout double. A double is more effective than an overcall of 2♣ since it gives partner the choice of trump suit and the hand isn't strong enough to overcall 2♣.

d) Pass. South has support for the unbid suits but, with only 9 high-card points, doesn't have enough strength for a takeout double, even adding 1 dummy point for the doubleton heart.

e) Double. With 12 high-card points plus 1 dummy point for the doubleton, South has enough strength for a takeout double. The three-card support for diamonds isn't ideal, but it's good enough.

f) Pass. South has 13 high-card points but doesn't have support for all the unbid suits. If South were to double and North chose spades as the trump suit, North-South would be poorly placed. Since South doesn't have a five-card suit, the hand is also unsuitable for an overcall. South passes and awaits developments.

g) Double. When the opponents have bid two suits, South can make a takeout double for the other two suits. South has support for hearts and clubs and, with 14 high-card points plus 1 dummy point for the doubleton spade, enough strength to compete for the contract.

h) Pass. South has 12 high-card points and could add 1 dummy point for the doubleton spade, but South needs to exercise some judgment when deciding whether to make a takeout double. South has only three-card support for hearts and much of the strength is in the opponents' suits. If South doubles, North will have to choose a suit at the two level and the partnership is likely to be much too high.

i) Double. There are only 11 high-card points but South can add three dummy points for the singleton spade and one for the doubleton diamond. That's enough to enter the auction. A takeout double is more flexible than an overcall in one of the suits since it gives partner a choice of two suits.

Quiz – Part II

East-West are vulnerable and North-South are non vulnerable. West opens 1♦, North doubles, and East passes. As advancer, what call would South make with the following hands?

WEST	NORTH	EAST	SOUTH
1♦	DOUBLE	PASS	?

a) ♠ 9 5
♥ 10 7 6 4 2
♦ J 7 3
♣ J 6 4

———

b) ♠ 8 6 4
♥ Q 7 3
♦ K Q 10 5
♣ A 7 2

———

c) ♠ K 6 3 2
♥ 8 4
♦ 6 5 3
♣ A 10 8 4

———

d) ♠ 6 2
♥ A Q 10 4 3
♦ 9 5 4
♣ K 8 4

———

e) ♠ 9 8 6
♥ K 5
♦ A K J 3
♣ K 7 5 2

———

f) ♠ A Q 7 5
♥ K Q J 3
♦ 8 3
♣ J 6 2

———

g) ♠ 8 6 3
♥ 9 5 4
♦ A Q 7 4
♣ J 6 2

———

h) ♠ 10 3 2
♥ Q 4
♦ 8 7 4
♣ K 8 7 6 5

———

i) ♠ A K J 7 4 2
♥ Q 3
♦ J 8 4
♣ 6 3

———

Answers to Quiz – Part II

a) 1♥. North has asked South to choose a trump suit and South can't pass if East doesn't bid. South bids the longest suit at the cheapest level.

b) 2NT. Here South has a balanced hand and 11 high-card points, with much of the strength in the opponents' suit. A jump to 2NT is invitational, showing about 11–12 points.

c) 1♠. With a choice of suits to bid, South prefers the major suit. Not only does it keep the auction lower in this situation, if the partnership has enough combined strength for a game contract, game in a major suit requires one less trick than in a minor suit.

d) 2♥. South wants to choose hearts as the trump suit but a bid at the cheapest level would show about 0–8 points. With 9 high-card points plus 1 length point for the five-card suit, South has enough to invite North to bid game with more than a minimum takeout double. South does this by jumping a level, to 2♥. Advancer's jump is not forcing, only invitational.

e) 3NT. With 14 high-card points, the partnership has enough combined strength for a game contract. With strength in the opponent's suit, it should be easier to take 9 tricks in a notrump contract than 11 tricks in a minor suit game of 5♣.

f) 2♦. The partnership has enough combined strength for a game contact. South has 13 high-card points and North has promised at least 13. The only question is WHERE? North may have four-card support for both hearts and spades but could have only three-card support for one of them. To get more information, South's only forcing bid is a cuebid of the opponents' suit. Over South's 2♦ advance, if North bids 2♥, South can raise to 4♥; if North bids 2♠, South can raise to 4♠.

g) 1NT. With a lot of strength in the opponents' suit and only three cards in each unbid suit, an advance of 1NT is the best choice. This shows about 6–10 points.

h) 2♣. Bidding the long suit at the cheapest level doesn't promise any strength, even at the two level. A new suit by advancer is not forcing.

i) 4♠. South has 11 high-card points plus 2 length points for the six-card suit. Since North is promising at least 13 points with the takeout double, the partnership should have enough combined strength for game. South knows spades will make an excellent trump suit since North promised support for spades. So, South has the information necessary to take the partnership to a game contract of 4♠.

Quiz – Part III

Both sides are vulnerable. East opens 1♦ and South makes a takeout double. West passes and North, as advancer, bids 1♠, showing about 0–8 points. East passes. What call would South make?

WEST	NORTH	EAST	SOUTH
		1♦	DOUBLE
PASS	1♠	PASS	?

a) ♠ Q J 7 3
   ♥ A Q J 8
   ♦ A 5
   ♣ K 10 4

b) ♠ K Q 8 3
   ♥ A J 8 4
   ♦ 7 3
   ♣ K 9 2

c) ♠ A K Q 5
   ♥ K J 7 2
   ♦ J
   ♣ Q J 7 3

East-West are non vulnerable; North-South are vulnerable. East opens 1♣, South doubles, West passes, and North jumps to 2♥, showing about 9–11 points as advancer. East passes. What call would South make?

WEST	NORTH	EAST	SOUTH
		1♣	DOUBLE
PASS	2♥	PASS	?

d) ♠ A J 8
   ♥ K Q 7 5
   ♦ K J 8 3
   ♣ K Q

e) ♠ A K 6 5
   ♥ J 10 8 3
   ♦ K Q 6 2
   ♣ 4

f) ♠ K Q 6 2
   ♥ Q 10 5
   ♦ A J 8 3
   ♣ 9 8

Neither side is vulnerable. East opens 1♦. What call would South make with the following hands?

WEST	NORTH	EAST	SOUTH
		1♦	?

g) ♠ K 9 7 5
   ♥ A Q 8 4
   ♦ 4
   ♣ K J 7 2

h) ♠ K 9 3
   ♥ A K J 7 3
   ♦ 10 7 6
   ♣ Q 7

i) ♠ K 9
   ♥ A K Q 9 7 5
   ♦ 9 3
   ♣ A Q 4

Answers to Quiz – Part III

a) 2♠. South has 17 high-card points plus 1 for the doubleton dia-
    mond, a total of 18. If North has 7 or 8 points, the partnership should
    have enough combined strength for game. South raises to 2♠ to show
    a medium-strength takeout double. North can pass with a very weak
    hand of about 0-6 points or move to game with 7 or 8.

b) Pass. With 13 high-card points plus 1 dummy point for the double-
    ton diamond, South has a minimum-strength hand for the takeout
    double. North may have no points and has at most about 8. The
    partnership is high enough.

c) 3♠. South has 17 high-card points plus 3 for the singleton diamond,
    for a total of 20. With a maximum-strength hand, South makes a
    highly invitational jump to 3♠. North can pass with about 0-4 points
    but continue to game with about 5-8 points.

d) 4♥. South has 19 high-card points plus 1 dummy point for the
    doubleton club. That's more than enough to accept North's invita-
    tion, but not enough to consider bidding any higher.

e) 4♥. South has 13 high-card points plus 3 dummy points for the
    singleton club. That's enough to accept North's invitational jump
    to 2♥ and go for the game bonus.

f) Pass. South has 12 high-card points plus 1 for the doubleton club.
    With a minimum for the takeout double, South declines North's
    invitational jump to 2♥. North has about 9-11 points, so partscore
    should be high enough.

g) Double. With 13 high-card points plus 3 dummy points for the
    singleton diamond and support for the unbid suits, South's hand is
    ideal for a takeout double.

h) 1♥. South has 13 high-card points. With a good five-card heart suit,
    the hand is more suitable for an overcall than a takeout double.

i) Double. South's distribution is more suitable for an overcall than a
    takeout double but South's hand is too strong for a simple overcall
    of 1♥. South has 18 high-card points plus 2 length points for the
    six-card suit, a total of 20. South would be disappointed if North
    passed, thinking South held at most about 17 points. So, South
    starts with a takeout double, a forcing bid. If North bids 1♠, for
    example, South will next bid 2♥, showing a hand too strong for a
    simple overcall of 1♥.

♠ Q 5
♥ A Q 10 9 4
♦ Q 5
♣ Q J 10 8

♠ 10 6 3
♥ J 8 2
♦ A 10 9 3
♣ K 3 2

NORTH

WEST   EAST

SOUTH

♠ A K 7 4
♥ 7 6
♦ K 6 4 2
♣ A 9 4

♠ J 9 8 2
♥ K 5 3
♦ J 8 7
♣ 7 6 5

Suggested Bidding

WEST	NORTH	EAST	SOUTH
	1♥	DOUBLE	PASS
2♦	PASS	PASS	PASS

North has 13 high-card points plus 1 length point for the five-card heart suit, enough to open 1♥.

East would have opened 1♦. After North's 1♥ opening, East can compete by making a takeout double. East has support for the three unbid suits, spades, diamonds, and clubs. East also has 14 high-card points and can add 1 dummy point for the doubleton heart.

South has only 5 high-card points, not enough to respond.

West has 8 high-card points. East has asked West to choose a trump suit other than hearts. West's longest suit is diamonds, so West bids diamonds at the cheapest available level, 2♦.

North has already described the hand by opening the bidding and passes with nothing extra to show.

Since West bid diamonds at the cheapest level, West has at most 8 points and could have zero. East knows the partnership is unlikely to have enough combined strength for a game contract and passes.

South passes[31] and the auction is over. The contract is 2♦.

---

[31] South might decide to compete to 2♥.

Suggested Opening Lead

North leads the ♣Q, top of the solid sequence.

Declarer's Plan

After North leads and dummy comes down, West makes a plan. West's goal is to take at least 8 tricks to make the 2♦ contract. West begins by counting the sure winners: two in spades, two in diamonds, and two in clubs for a total of six. Two more tricks are required.

Moving to the second stage, West browses Declarer's Checklist. The diamond suit offers a chance to develop an extra trick through length. There are eight combined diamonds

```
┌─── DECLARER'S PLAN—THE ABC'S ───

  Declarer: West      Contract: 2♦

  ASSESS THE SITUATION
  Goal                      8
  Sure Tricks               6
  Extra Tricks Needed   2

  BROWSE DECLARER'S CHECKLIST
  Promotion:
  Length                    1 in diamonds
  The Finesse
  Trumping in Dummy   1 in hearts

  CONSIDER THE ORDER
  • Draw trumps.
  • Develop the extra diamond trick
    early.
  • Keep one trump in dummy to ruff
    a heart.
```

in the East and West hands. If the missing diamonds divide 3-2, declarer can create an extra winner in that suit. Since declarer has more hearts than dummy, there is also a chance to gain a trick by ruffing one of declarer's hearts with one of dummy's trumps.

After winning club trick, declarer draws trumps by playing the ♦A and ♦K. If declarer then leads a third round of diamonds, giving up a trick to South's ♦J[32], declarer's remaining diamonds are winners.

To ruff a heart in dummy, declarer has to first lose two heart tricks to the defenders. Then dummy will be void in hearts and West's remaining heart can be ruffed with one of East's diamonds.

Comments

By using the takeout double, East-West find their diamond fit and reach a successful partscore contract despite the opening 1♥ bid. If North-South compete to 2♥, that contract can be defeated two tricks.

---

[32] Declarer doesn't actually need to lead a third round of diamonds. Declarer can leave the ♦J outstanding and let South take a trick with it whenever South chooses.

DEAL: 10

DEALER: EAST

VUL: N-S

♠ 7 2
♥ Q J 10 9 5
♦ K Q
♣ Q 10 8 2

NORTH

WEST   EAST

SOUTH

♠ A 8 6 3
♥ 7 4
♦ 9 5 4 2
♣ 6 5 3

♠ Q J 10
♥ K 2
♦ A J 8 7 6 3
♣ 9 4

♠ K 9 5 4
♥ A 8 6 3
♦ 10
♣ A K J 7

Suggested Bidding

WEST	NORTH	EAST	SOUTH
		1♦	DOUBLE
PASS	2♥	PASS	4♥
PASS	PASS	PASS	

East has 11 high-card points plus 2 points for the six-card diamond suit. With enough to open the bidding, East starts with the long minor suit, 1♦.

With 15 high-card points and support for all of the unbid suits, South would like to compete for the contract. South can add 3 dummy points for the singleton heart, to bring the total to 18. By making a takeout double, South shows at least the values for an opening bid and asks North to choose the suit.

West has only 4 high-card points, not enough to respond. West passes.

Asked to choose a trump suit, North knows WHERE, hearts. North has 10 high-card points plus 1 length point for the five-card suit. Since South has promised at least 13 points, North jumps to 2♥ to show an invitational hand of about 9-11 points. Since North was forced to bid, an advance to the minimum level of 1♥ would show only 0–8 points.

East, having opened the bidding, has nothing extra to show.

South has 18 points, more than enough to accept North's invitational jump to 2♥. South knows How High, and takes the partnership to game. After everyone passes, North is declarer in 4♥.

Suggested Opening Lead

East leads the ♠Q, top of the solid sequence, against North's 4♥.

Declarer's Plan

North's goal is to take at least ten tricks to make the 4♥ contract. North begins by counting the sure winners: one heart and four clubs for a total of five tricks. Five more tricks are required.

South browses Declarer's Checklist. Declarer can promote a diamond winner by driving out the ♦A.

Declarer can hope that East holds the ♠A and that dummy's ♠K will become a winner

DECLARER'S PLAN—THE ABC'S
Declarer: North   Contract: 4♥
ASSESS THE SITUATION
Goal 10
Sure Tricks 5
Extra Tricks Needed 5
BROWSE DECLARER'S CHECKLIST
Promotion: 1 in diamonds
Length
The Finesse 4 in hearts
Trumping in Dummy
CONSIDER THE ORDER
• Be in the right place at the right time to lead a heart and capture East's ♥K.

through the finesse. That doesn't work on the actual deal.

Declarer could promote three extra winners in hearts by driving out the ♥K, but that isn't good enough. Instead, declarer must use the concept of the finesse to take all the tricks in hearts without losing a trick to East's ♥K. Declarer does this by leading the ♥Q (or ♥J, ♥10, or ♥9) from the North hand. If East plays the ♥K, South's ♥A wins and declarer takes the rest of the heart tricks. If East doesn't play the ♥K on North's ♥Q, declarer plays low from dummy and the ♥Q wins. As long as East holds the ♥K, declarer's finesse succeeds.

Comments

North-South manage to reach a game contract in their best trump suit despite the opening bid by East. South makes use of the takeout double and North cooperates by choosing the suit and showing a hand of invitational strength.

DEAL: 11

DEALER: SOUTH
VUL: E-W

NORTH
♠ Q 10 3
♥ 10 7 6
♦ 7 5 4 3
♣ J 8 2

WEST
♠ 9 6
♥ A 9 5 2
♦ K J 10
♣ A 9 7 4

EAST
♠ 8 4 2
♥ K Q J 8 3
♦ A Q 8
♣ 5 3

SOUTH
♠ A K J 7 5
♥ 4
♦ 9 6 2
♣ K Q 10 6

Suggested Bidding

WEST	NORTH	EAST	SOUTH
			1♠
DOUBLE	PASS	4♥	PASS
PASS	PASS		

South has 13 high-card points plus 1 for the five-card suit. South opens 1♠, the five-card major suit.

West has only 12 high-card points but can add 1 dummy point for the doubleton spade when considering making a takeout double of the opening bid. With 13 points plus support for the unbid suits, West makes a takeout double.

North, with only 3 high-card points, doesn't have enough to respond.

East has a definite preference for hearts as the trump suit. So, East knows WHERE. In addition, East has 12 high-card points plus 1 length point for the five-card suit for a total of 13. Since West is promising at least 13 points for the takeout double, East also knows HOW HIGH. The partnership has enough combined strength for a game contract. Putting this together, East takes the partnership right to a game contract with hearts as trumps, 4♥.

South, West, and North have nothing more to add, so East becomes declarer in a 4♥ contract.

Suggested Opening Lead

South leads the ♠A, top of the touching high cards, against East's 4♥ contract. The ♣K, top of the touching high cards in that suit, would also be a reasonable choice.

Declarer's Plan

Declarer makes a plan for playing the hand. East's goal is to take at least ten tricks. East can count on five tricks from the heart suit, three in diamonds, and one in clubs. That's a total of nine tricks. One more trick is required.

Moving to the second stage, South browses Declarer's Checklist. Since there are more spades in declarer's hand than in the dummy, declarer can plan to gain a trick by ruffing a spade loser in the dummy.

┌─── DECLARER'S PLAN—THE ABC'S ───┐

Declarer: East   Contract: 4♥

ASSESS THE SITUATION
Goal   10
Sure Tricks   9
Extra Tricks Needed   1

BROWSE DECLARER'S CHECKLIST
Promotion:
Length
The Finesse
Trumping in Dummy   1 in spades

CONSIDER THE ORDER
- Draw trumps first.
- Take the losses early.
- Keep a trump in dummy to ruff a spade.

Suppose South wins the ♠A and then decides to lead the ♣K to promote a winner in that suit. Declarer wins the ♣A and can start by drawing trumps. It takes three rounds of hearts to draw all the defenders hearts, but there is still one trump left in the dummy. It is then perfectly safe for declarer to take the diamond winners. Declarer must then be willing to give up a spade trick to the opponents. That leaves declarer in a position to trump the remaining spade with dummy's last heart. The defenders get only two spade tricks and one club trick.

Comments

East and West are able to reach their game contract in hearts after South's opening bid of 1♠ by effectively using the takeout double. It is important that East take the partnership all the way to the game level. If East made a minimum advance of 2♥, or even an invitational jump to 3♥, West would pass, holding a minimum for the takeout double. The game contract would be missed.

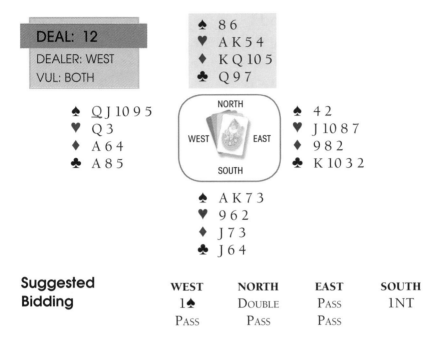

		DEAL: 12
		DEALER: WEST
		VUL: BOTH

NORTH
♠ 8 6
♥ A K 5 4
♦ K Q 10 5
♣ Q 9 7

WEST
♠ Q J 10 9 5
♥ Q 3
♦ A 6 4
♣ A 8 5

EAST
♠ 4 2
♥ J 10 8 7
♦ 9 8 2
♣ K 10 3 2

SOUTH
♠ A K 7 3
♥ 9 6 2
♦ J 7 3
♣ J 6 4

Suggested Bidding

WEST	NORTH	EAST	SOUTH
1♠	DOUBLE	PASS	1NT
PASS	PASS	PASS	

West has 13 high-card points plus 1 length point for the five-card suit. West opens 1♠.

North has support for the unbid suits—hearts, diamonds, and clubs—and can value the hand as 14 high-card points plus 1 dummy point for the doubleton spade. North makes a takeout double.

East, with only 4 high-card points, passes.

South has 9 high-card points and doesn't have four or more cards in any of the unbid suits. With so much strength in spades, however, South can bid 1NT, suggesting notrump as the best choice of contract.

West, North, and East have nothing more to add, so the contract becomes 1NT with South as declarer.

Suggested Opening Lead

West leads the ♠Q, top of the solid sequence, against South's 1NT contract.

Declarer's Plan

South is declarer and the goal is to take seven tricks with no trump suit. South counts two sure tricks in spades and two in hearts. Three more tricks need to be developed.

South browses Declarer's Checklist. Three tricks can be promoted in diamonds by driving out the ♦A. That's enough to make the contract.

After winning the first spade trick, declarer should go about promoting the extra winners in diamonds, taking the losses early. Declarer can start with the ♦J, high card from the short side, and continue leading diamonds until the defenders take their ♦A. On regaining the lead, declarer can take the established diamond winners to go with the spade and heart winners.

> **DECLARER'S PLAN—THE ABC'S**
>
> Declarer: South   Contract: 1NT
>
> **ASSESS THE SITUATION**
> | | |
> |---|---|
> | Goal | 7 |
> | Sure Tricks | 4 |
> | Extra Tricks Needed | 3 |
>
> **BROWSE DECLARER'S CHECKLIST**
> | | |
> |---|---|
> | Promotion: | 3 in diamonds |
> | Length | |
> | The Finesse | |
> | Trumping in Dummy | |
>
> **CONSIDER THE ORDER**
> - Take the losses early.

Comments

If declarer takes the heart and spade winners before giving up a diamond trick to the defenders, the contract can be defeated. East-West will have eight established winners to take: three spade tricks, two heart tricks, a diamond, and two club tricks.

When you don't think the contract belongs to your side, strive to compete to the level of the number of trumps held by your partnership.

—LARRY COHEN, FOLLOWING THE LAW (1994)

The Competitive Auction

When the opponents aren't bidding, your objective during the auction is straightforward: to reach the best contract by deciding How High and Where the partnership belongs. In a competitive auction, the objective can change. To prevent the opponents from buying the contract, you may have to bid higher than you would like or you may want to take preemptive action to prevent the opponents from reaching their best contract. Also, in a competitive auction, new calls become available to help you bid effectively.

Everyone at the table is affected by competitive bids: responder, advancer, opener, and even the overcaller or takeout doubler. Let's start by looking at the impact on responder when the opponents intervene.

Responder's Action After an Overcall

If North opens the bidding and East makes an overcall, South is still the responder.

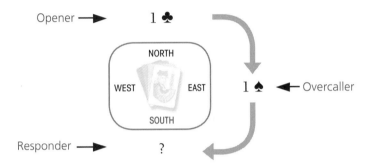

Sometimes the overcall won't affect the call South was planning to make; sometimes, only a minor adjustment is needed; and sometimes there will be a large impact and South must consider other options. Let's look at each scenario in turn.

NO CHANGE

North opens the bidding 1♦ and East overcalls 1♥. It's South's call.

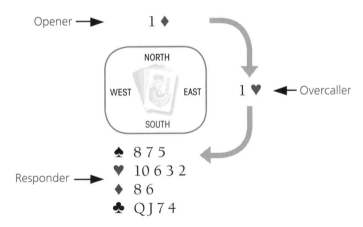

Pass. With only 3 high-card points, South was planning to pass North's opening bid. East's 1♥ overcall doesn't affect the decision.

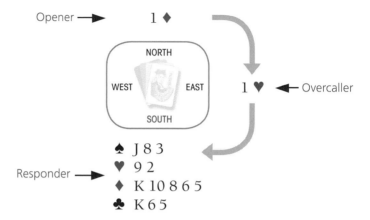

Opener ➡ 1 ♦

NORTH
WEST   EAST   1 ♥ ⬅ Overcaller
SOUTH

♠ J 8 3
Responder ➡ ♥ 9 2
♦ K 10 8 6 5
♣ K 6 5

2♦. South was planning to raise partner's diamonds to the two level, showing 6-10 points. The overcall doesn't prevent South from raising to 2♦ to show the diamond support.

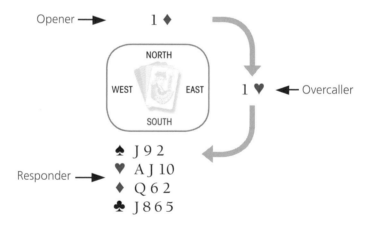

Opener ➡ 1 ♦

NORTH
WEST   EAST   1 ♥ ⬅ Overcaller
SOUTH

♠ J 9 2
Responder ➡ ♥ A J 10
♦ Q 6 2
♣ J 8 6 5

1NT. If East passed, South would respond 1NT, showing about 6-10 points. South can make the same bid after the 1♥ overcall. However, it's a good idea to have some strength in the overcalled suit when bidding notrump. The opponents will likely lead hearts to try to develop enough tricks to defeat the contract.

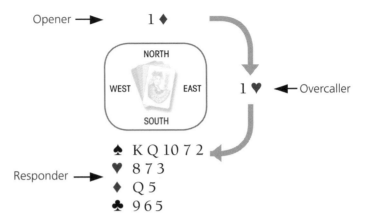

Opener ⟶ 1 ♦

NORTH

WEST   EAST

SOUTH

1 ♥ ⟵ Overcaller

Responder ⟶

♠ K Q 10 7 2
♥ 8 7 3
♦ Q 5
♣ 9 6 5

1♠. South would have responded 1♠ if East had passed. Nothing prevents South from making the same bid. A new suit by responder is still forcing after an overcall and shows 6 or more points.

MINOR ADJUSTMENT

North opens the bidding 1♣ and East overcalls 1♠. It's South's call.

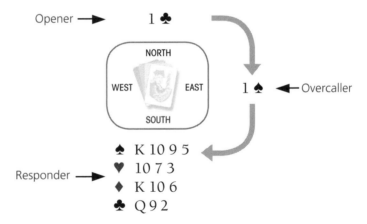

Opener ⟶ 1 ♣

NORTH

WEST   EAST

SOUTH

1 ♠ ⟵ Overcaller

Responder ⟶

♠ K 10 9 5
♥ 10 7 3
♦ K 10 6
♣ Q 9 2

1NT. South would have responded 1♠, showing 6 or more points and four or more spades, if East had passed. Now that East has taken away that bid, 1NT is a reasonable compromise with 8 high-card points and some strength in spades.

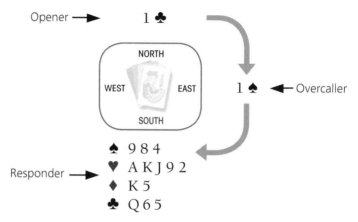

Opener → 1♣

Overcaller → 1♠

Responder →
♠ 9 8 4
♥ A K J 9 2
♦ K 5
♣ Q 6 5

2♥. South would have responded 1♥ if East passed. That would show four or more hearts and at least 6 points, although South could have a much stronger hand. 1♥ is no longer available after the 1♠ overcall, but South has enough strength to bid a new suit at the two level, showing five or more hearts and about 11 or more points.

LARGE IMPACT

North opens the bidding 1♦ and East overcalls 2♣. Let's look at South's decision.

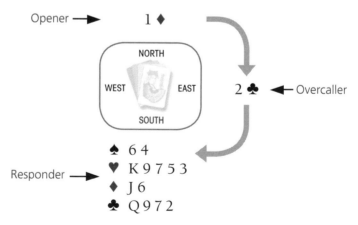

Opener → 1♦

Overcaller → 2♣

Responder →
♠ 6 4
♥ K 9 7 5 3
♦ J 6
♣ Q 9 7 2

Pass. South was planning to respond 1♥ but can no longer make that bid after the 2♣ overcall. With only 6 high-card points, South doesn't have enough strength to bid a new suit at the two level. That would promise about 11 or more points and would be forcing. The partnership could get much too high.

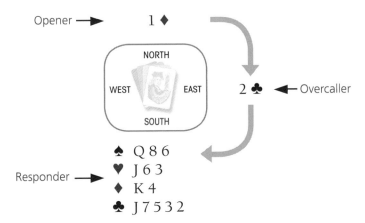

Pass. South would have responded 1NT, showing about 6-10 points, if East had passed. After the 2♣ overcall, South doesn't have enough strength to bid 2NT, which would show an invitational hand of about 11-12 points. Instead, South passes for now. The auction isn't over. North will get another chance to bid and can take some action with extra strength or a suitable hand for competing further. So, it is unlikely North-South will miss a game contract if there is one.

OTHER OPTIONS

The opponents' overcall also provides the following options:

- Responder's preemptive jump raise
- Responder's cuebid
- Responder's double

Responder's Preemptive Jump Raise

Preemptive bids are frequently used in competitive auctions because they make it difficult for the opponents to find their best contract. When right-hand opponent overcalls and responder has four-card or longer support for opener's suit but a weak hand of about 6–9 points[33], preemptive action becomes a priority. Responder can make a preemptive jump raise using the following guideline:

> ### Responder's Preemptive Jump Raise with Support and 6-9 Points
>
> * 4-card support   Jump to the three level.
> * 5-card support   Jump to the game level.

For example, consider South's call on the following hands after North opens 1♥ and East overcalls 1♠.

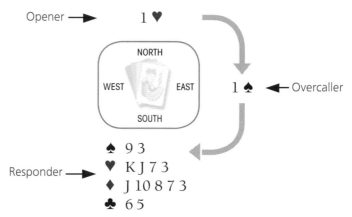

Opener ⟶   1 ♥

NORTH

WEST   EAST   1 ♠ ⟵ Overcaller

SOUTH

♠ 9 3
Responder ⟶ ♥ K J 7 3
♦ J 10 8 7 3
♣ 6 5

3♥. With 5 high-card points plus 1 dummy point for each doubleton, South would raise to 2♥ showing three-card or longer support and 6–9 points if East passed. Once the auction becomes competitive, it is more important to show the fit and also try to keep the opponents out of the auction. A jump to 3♥ is preemptive[34].

---

[33] 6–9 points is a guideline. Some players make a preemptive jump raise with fewer than 6 points.

[34] Some partnerships prefer to keep the jump raise after an overcall as invitational—a limit raise—after an overcall.

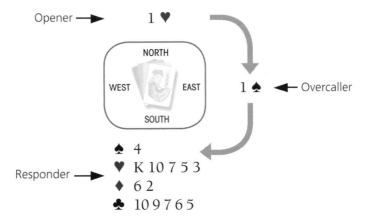

Opener ➝ 1 ♥

NORTH
WEST   EAST   1 ♠ ⬅ Overcaller
SOUTH

Responder ➝
♠ 4
♥ K 10 7 5 3
♦ 6 2
♣ 10 9 7 6 5

4♥. With five-card support and a weak hand, South can make a preemptive raise all the way to the four level. South doesn't expect North to make 4♥, although that's a possibility when South has such excellent trump support and an unbalanced hand with a singleton and doubleton. South expects the opponents can likely make a game unless North has a very good hand. The preemptive jump raise should make it more challenging for East-West to get to their best contract[35].

With only three-card support, responder doesn't make a preemptive raise.

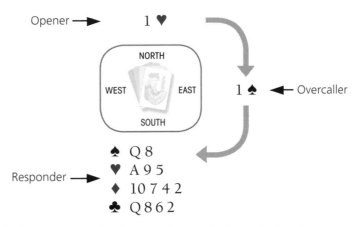

Opener ➝ 1 ♥

NORTH
WEST   EAST   1 ♠ ⬅ Overcaller
SOUTH

Responder ➝
♠ Q 8
♥ A 9 5
♦ 10 7 4 2
♣ Q 8 6 2

[35] See Practice Deal #22 for an example of responder's preemptive jump raise in action.

2♥. With three-card support for North's suit, South settles for a single raise to the two level. That might be the best spot for North-South and there's no reason to expect that the opponents can make a game when South has such a balanced hand with high cards in spades and clubs.

Responder's Cuebid

Since the opponents' overcall shows a good five-card or longer suit, responder isn't going to want to suggest the opponents' suit as the trump suit. So, responder can use a bid of the opponents' suit, a cuebid, as an artificial forcing bid.

When partner opens in a suit at the one level and the next player overcalls, responder's cuebid of the opponents' suit shows support for opener's suit and a hand of at least invitational strength—11 or more points[36].

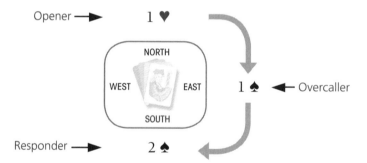

Responder's Cuebid

Responder's cuebid is a forcing bid showing:
- Support for opener's suit, three cards or more.
- At least invitational strength (11+).

---

[36] Replacing the limit raise with the cuebid is what allows responder to use the jump raise as preemptive after an overcall. See Practice Deal #20 for an example of responder's cuebid in action.

SUPPORT FOR OPENER'S SUIT

Ideally, responder's cuebid shows four-card or longer support for opener's suit. With three-card support and 11 or more points, responder usually bids a new suit, planning to show the support at the next opportunity.

INVITATIONAL STRENGTH OR BETTER

Responder's cuebid shows 11 or more points and support for opener's suit. With 11-12 points, responder will pass if opener makes a minimum rebid of the suit; with 13 or more points, responder will continue to game even if opener's rebid describes a minimum hand.

For example, North opens 1♥ and East overcalls 1♠. It's South's call.

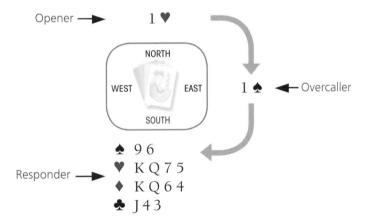

2♠. With 11 high-card points plus 1 dummy point for the doubleton spade, South would have made a limit raise to 3♥ if East had passed. When East overcalls 1♠, South shows this type of hand with a cuebid of 2♠. With more than a minimum opening bid, North will accept the invitation by bidding 4♥. With a minimum opening bid, North will reject the invitation by rebidding 3♥ and South will pass.

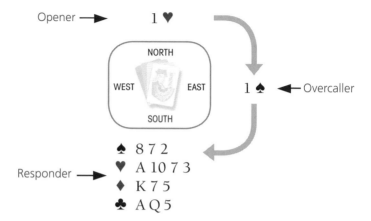

Opener → 1 ♥

NORTH

WEST   EAST   1 ♠ ← Overcaller

SOUTH

Responder →
♠ 8 7 2
♥ A 10 7 3
♦ K 7 5
♣ A Q 5

2♠. With 13 high-card points and four-card heart support, South starts with a cuebid of spades, the opponents' suit. Even if North shows a minimum opening bid, South will take the partnership to game by bidding 4♥. An immediate jump to 4♥ by South would be a preemptive jump raise, showing a weak hand.

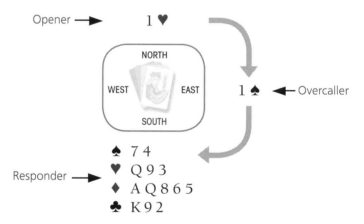

Opener → 1 ♥

NORTH

WEST   EAST   1 ♠ ← Overcaller

SOUTH

Responder →
♠ 7 4
♥ Q 9 3
♦ A Q 8 6 5
♣ K 9 2

2♦. With only three-card heart support and 11 or more points, South starts by bidding a new suit, planning to raise hearts at the next opportunity. A cuebid usually promises at least four-card support.

Responder's Double – The Negative Double

At one time, the double of an opponents' overcall by responder was treated as a penalty double. The modern style is to use responder's double for takeout, similar to the takeout double of an opponents' opening bid. To distinguish responder's double from a standard takeout double, responder's double is referred to as a *negative double*. The term 'negative' means not for penalty.

A double by responder is for takeout when partner opens the bidding at the one level in a suit and the next player overcalls a suit at the one, two, or three level[37]:

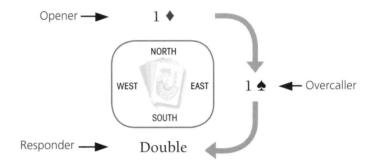

Responder's Negative Double

- Support for both unbid suits.
- Enough strength to compete.

SUPPORT FOR THE UNBID SUITS

Since opener has bid one suit and the opponent on responder's right has overcalled in another suit, there will always be two unbid suits. Responder ideally has four-card support for each unbid suit[38].

---

[37] Some partnerships use the negative double only when an opponent overcalls at the one or two level.

[38] In practice, responder can sometimes get away without support for an unbid minor suit, provided responder has the strength and distribution to bid something else if opener bids the minor suit.

STRENGTH TO COMPETE

The strength responder needs to make a negative double depends on the level that opener will be forced to bid. If there is room for opener to bid one of responder's suits at the one or two level, responder needs only about 6 or more points. If opener may have to bid at the three level, responder needs about 9 or more points; if opener may have to bid at the four level, responder will need about 11 or more points.

Here are examples of hands for responder's double, the negative double. North opens the bidding 1♦, East overcalls 1♠, and it's South's call.

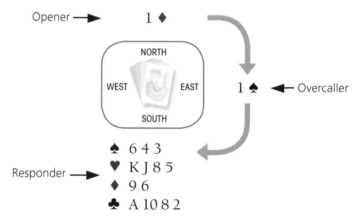

Double. If East hadn't overcalled, South could have responded 1♥, showing four or more hearts and 6 or more points. East's 1♠ overcall presents a challenge. South doesn't have support for diamonds, doesn't have enough strength in spades to bid 1NT, and doesn't have enough strength to bid a new suit at the two level, which would show about 11 or more points. This is an ideal hand for the negative double.

South's double describes a hand with support for both the unbid suits, hearts and clubs. If North now bids 2♥ or 2♣, South will pass, having found a suitable trump fit. If North doesn't have four cards in hearts or clubs and rebids 1NT or 2♦, South will also pass, settling for partscore.

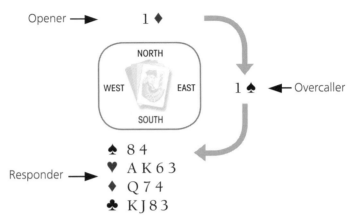

Opener ⟶ 1 ♦

Overcaller ⟶ 1 ♠

Responder ⟶
♠ 8 4
♥ A K 6 3
♦ Q 7 4
♣ K J 8 3

Double. Although there is enough strength to bid a new suit at the two level, South can start with the negative double to show support for both unbid suits. With 13 high-card points, South plans to get to game. If North bids 2♥, for example, South will raise to 4♥, putting the partnership in game in the eight-card major suit fit.

Here are examples of hands that are unsuitable for the negative double. North opens 1♥ and East overcalls 2♦.

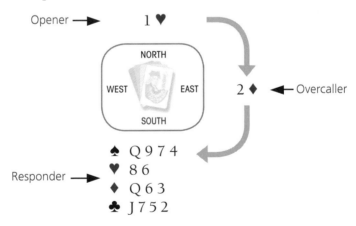

Opener ⟶ 1 ♥

Overcaller ⟶ 2 ♦

Responder ⟶
♠ Q 9 7 4
♥ 8 6
♦ Q 6 3
♣ J 7 5 2

Pass. South has support for both the unbid suits, spades and clubs but, with only 5 high-card points, there isn't enough strength to compete. If North chooses to bid clubs, for example, it will have to be at the three level and the partnership will be much too high if North has a minimum opening bid.

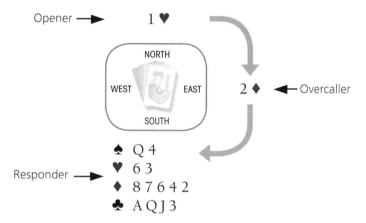

Opener ➔   1 ♥

2 ♦ ◀— Overcaller

♠ Q 4
Responder ➔   ♥ 6 3
♦ 8 7 6 4 2
♣ A Q J 3

Pass. With 9 high-card points, there is enough strength to compete at the two level, but South doesn't have support for both unbid suits. If North were to bid 2♠, the partnership would be in a poor contract.

Responder's Action After a Takeout Double

When right-hand opponent doubles partner's opening bid for take-out, no bidding room is taken up. It would seem that responder could make the same call as if there were no double. In practice, the auction has become competitive, so the priority for the partnership has changed. Since right-hand opponent's takeout double has shown the equivalent of an opening bid, there is less chance that the partnership is headed for a game contract. The focus shifts to trying to buy the contract or keeping the opponents from reaching their best contract—similar to the situation for responder after an overcall.

Responder's actions are affected because a new call is available after a takeout double, the *redouble*[39]. You can redouble only after your side has been doubled.

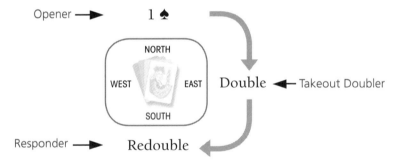

The redouble was originally introduced as a way to increase the score when one side is doubled for penalties. Since a takeout double is not for penalty, however, the redouble can be put to another use.

---

[39] The redouble is the last call you need to learn. The only allowable calls in the game are the suit and notrump bids from the one to the seven level, pass, double, and redouble.

Responder's Redouble

When partner's opening bid is doubled for takeout, a redouble by responder essentially says, "I think the contract belongs to our side." If the opening bid is in a suit at the one level, use the following guideline when the opponent on your right doubles:

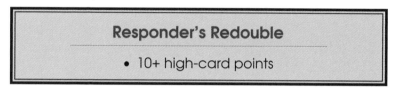

Responder's Redouble

- 10+ high-card points

Here are examples of responder's use of the redouble. North opens the bidding 1♠, East doubles, and it's South's call.

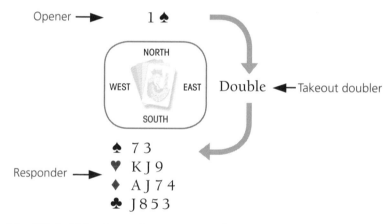

Opener → 1 ♠

NORTH

WEST   EAST   Double ← Takeout doubler

SOUTH

Responder →
♠ 7 3
♥ K J 9
♦ A J 7 4
♣ J 8 5 3

Redouble. With 10 high-card points, South starts with a redouble. It tells partner the deal belongs to North-South. When the opponents bid, South may choose to double the East-West contract for penalty[40] or continue bidding to North-South's best contract.

---

[40] See Practice Deal #24 for an example of starting with a redouble and then doubling the opponents' contract for penalty.

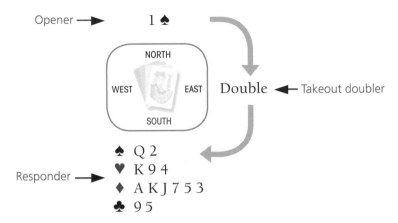

Opener ——▶ 1 ♠

NORTH

WEST   EAST   Double ◀—— Takeout doubler

SOUTH

♠ Q 2
Responder ——▶ ♥ K 9 4
♦ A K J 7 5 3
♣ 9 5

Redouble. With 13 high-card points plus 2 length points, South would have responded 2♦ if East had passed. The new suit response would be forcing and South would plan to eventually make sure North-South gets to at least game. When East doubles, South first redoubles to show 10 or more high-card points. If the opponents now bid 2♣, for example, South plans to bid 2♦ and the partnership can continue bidding as if there had been no interference.

Responder's redouble shows about 10 or more points but could be based on a variety of hands. Responder might have a balanced hand, a long suit, or support for opener's suit. As a guideline, opener usually passes the redouble, waiting to see which type of hand responder holds.

The Impact of the Redouble

The impact of having the redouble available is that responder's other responses that would typically show about 10 or more points can now be used to show weaker hands. Here are examples of how the availability of the redouble can affect responder's choices. North opens the bidding 1♠ and East doubles for takeout.

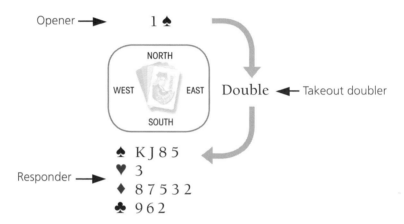

3♠. With 4 high-card points plus 3 dummy points for the singleton heart, South would raise to only 2♠ if East passed. After the takeout double, a jump raise by responder is preemptive. With enough strength to make a limit raise, showing 11-12 points, South could have started with a redouble.

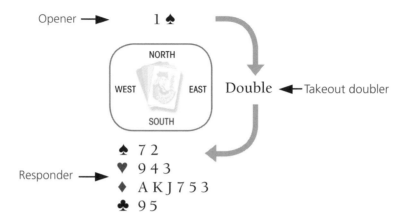

2♦. If East had passed, South would have to respond 1NT because there isn't enough strength to bid a new suit at the two level. After the takeout double, South can afford to respond 2♦. North can draw the inference that South has fewer than 10 high-card points because South didn't redouble[41]. A new suit response at the two level is not forcing after a takeout double[42].

Effective use of the redouble requires good cooperation between opener and responder and is a little beyond the scope of this book. It's introduced here so you will be aware that it exists and to see how the meaning of responder's bids can change in a competitive auction.

---

[41] See Practice Deal # 23 for an example.

[42] For reasons beyond the scope of this text, most partnerships continue to treat a new suit response at the one level as forcing after a takeout double.

Advancer's Action in a Competitive Auction

Previous chapters discussed advancer's actions when partner made an overcall or takeout double and responder passed. Let's look at the impact on advancer if responder bids.

Advancing an Overcall if Responder Bids

When partner makes an overcall and responder bids or doubles, there won't usually be much effect on your call. Partner's overcall isn't forcing, so you don't have to bid. However, the overcall has invited you into the auction, so you should be willing to compete for the auction.

West opens the bidding 1♥, North overcalls 1♠, and East bids 2♥. It's South's call as advancer.

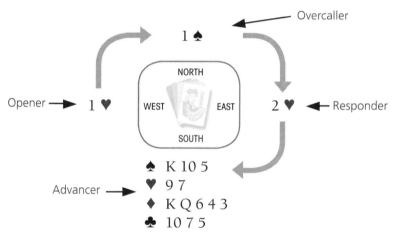

2♠. With three-card support for partner's suit and 8 high-card points, South would have raised to 2♠ if East had passed. East's 2♥ bid doesn't stop South from making the same call.

A more challenging situation would be if East raised to 3♥ instead of 2♥. Now South can no longer make a comfortable bid of 2♠. South has to decide between passing and making the slight overbid of 3♠. Of course, that is one of the reasons East may have jumped to 3♥ with a weak hand…to present South with a challenge. There's no right answer. Competitive bidding decisions are part of what makes the game so interesting.

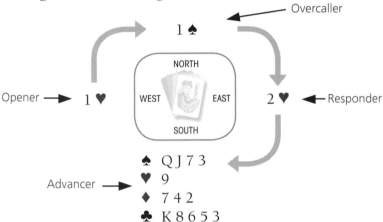

3♠. A jump raise of partner's overcall is still preemptive. This is similar to responder's actions in a competitive auction. With enough strength to make an invitational raise of partner's suit, South would make a cuebid of 3♥.

Advancing a Takeout Double if Responder Bids

When partner makes a takeout double, you are in a different situation than when partner overcalls. If the opponent on your right passes, you are expected to bid something.

Things change when the opponent on your right bids after partner's takeout double. You are no longer forced to bid. However, the takeout double has invited you into the auction, so you want to compete whenever possible.

West opens 1♦, North doubles, and East raises to 2♦. It's South's call.

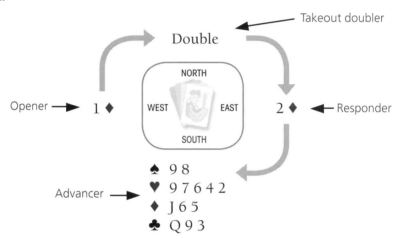

Pass. If East had passed, South would have bid 1♥. South couldn't pass and leave the partnership defending against 1♦ doubled. North wants to play with any suit as trumps except diamonds. Once East bids, South can pass with a weak hand, leaving the contract to East-West unless North bids again.

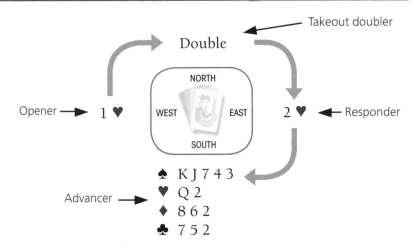

2♠. If East had passed, South would bid only 1♠ with this hand as advancer. South has only 6 high-card points plus 1 length point for the five-card suit. A jump to 2♠ would be invitational, showing about 9-11 points. When East raises, South doesn't have to bid but North showed interest in entering the auction and South has enough to compete. Bidding 2♠ doesn't show too much. With an invitational hand of about 9-11, South could jump to 3♠. With more strength, South could cuebid 3♥ the opponents' suit.

If East were to make a preemptive jump to 3♥, South would probably pass. South doesn't have quite enough to compete at the three level. North would expect a little more. Again, you can see the challenge presented by an opponent's preemptive jump raise.

Opener's Action in a Competitive Auction

After you open the bidding, the auction can proceed in many ways, especially if the opponent on your left overcalls. Your partner, responder, might make a negative double or a cuebid, and you must choose an appropriate rebid. As opener, you can also make use of competitive calls such as the double.

Here are some examples of West's rebid in a competitive auction after opening the bidding.

WEST	NORTH	EAST	SOUTH
1♦	1♠	DOUBLE	PASS
?			

♠ A 8 3
♥ Q 7 5 2
♦ A J 9 8
♣ K 5

2♥. East has made a negative double, showing enough strength to compete and support for the unbid suits, hearts and clubs. With four hearts, West knows there is a fit in hearts. With a minimum opening bid, West bids hearts at the cheapest level, 2♥. In effect, it is as though East responded 1♥ and West raised to 2♥.

With a medium-strength opening bid of about 17-18 points, West would jump to 3♥, inviting East to bid game with more than about 6 or 7 points. With a maximum-strength opening bid of about 19-21 points, West would jump all the way to a game contract.

WEST	NORTH	EAST	SOUTH
1♥	1♠	2♠	PASS
?			

♠ Q 9 7
♥ K J 6 5 2
♦ A 8 3
♣ Q 8

3♥. East's cuebid of the overcalled suit shows support for hearts and a hand with 11 or more points. With a minimum opening bid, West bids 3♥. If West had about 15 or more points,

West would jump to game, 4♥. After the 3♥ bid, East will pass with 11-12. With a stronger hand, East will bid again.

WEST	NORTH	EAST	SOUTH
1♠	DOUBLE	3♠	PASS
?			

♠ A Q 7 6 3
♥ K 4
♦ K Q 8 5
♣ Q 8

Pass. East's jump raise after the takeout double is preemptive. West has more than a minimum opening bid but, based on East's weakness, West would pass.

WEST	NORTH	EAST	SOUTH
1♦	1♥	PASS	2♥
?			

♠ A K 10 8
♥ 6
♦ K Q 8 5
♣ A Q J 6

Double. Although East passed after the opening bid and North's overcall, West has enough strength to want to compete for the contract. A double by West at this point is for takeout. West wants East to choose any trump suit other than hearts.

Action After Making an Overcall
or Takeout Double

When you make an overcall or a takeout double, it is usually up to your partner, advancer, to decide How High to compete. However, you may need to act again with extra strength or distribution, or if advancer makes a forcing bid. Here are some examples of West's actions after South opens 1♦.

WEST	NORTH	EAST	SOUTH
			1♦
1♠	2♦	3♦	PASS
?			

♠ A J 10 9 7 5
♥ A 4
♦ 7 3
♣ K Q 5

4♠. East's cuebid shows a hand with at least 11 points. With more than a minimum overcall and a good suit, West can jump to 4♠. With a minimum overcall, West would bid 3♠.

WEST	NORTH	EAST	SOUTH
			1♦
DOUBLE	2♦	PASS	PASS
?			

♠ A Q 10 9
♥ A K J 5
♦ 4
♣ K J 9 5

Double. After West's initial takeout double, North raised opener's suit and East passed. East probably doesn't have much. However, West's hand is strong enough to want to compete further. West can make a second takeout double to again ask East to choose a trump suit other than diamonds.

The Penalty Double

Although the double is frequently used to ask partner to bid, it can also be used as a penalty double. A penalty double increases the score for defeating the opponents' contract and the size of the penalty depends on the opponents' vulnerability, as discussed in Chapter 1.

The penalty double prevents the opponents from frivolously bidding too much to prevent you from buying the contract. For example, suppose you can make a vulnerable game contract of 4♥. At duplicate or Chicago bridge, this would be worth 620 points. If the opponents were non vulnerable and the penalty double didn't exist, they could go down 10 tricks and only lose 500 points (10 x 50). The penalty double is a deterrent against overbidding. It doesn't stop the opponents from taking a calculated sacrifice to prevent you from bidding and making your game contract, but it does limit their overbidding.

The downside to doubling for penalty is that the opponents will receive an increased score if they make their contract. The trick score will be doubled and they will get a bonus of 50 points for making the contract. There is also a large bonus for making doubled overtricks (see Appendix 2)[43].

It is risky to double the opponents in a partscore contract unless you are certain you can defeat them. If they make their partscore, the trick score is doubled and, if the total is 100 or more points, they now get a game bonus.

---

[43] In addition, the opponents can redouble if they think they can make their contract. That increases the trick score two-fold, but also the penalties if the contract is defeated.

Takeout or Penalty?

Since the double is sometimes used for takeout and sometimes for penalty, the challenge is to know when a double is for takeout and when it is for penalty. A detailed discussion of this topic is outside the scope of this book. For now, a reasonable agreement is:

Distinguishing Penalty Doubles from Takeout Doubles

- Doubles of the opponents' 1NT or 2NT opening bids are for penalty.
- Doubles of the opponents' bids at the game level or higher are for penalty.

Here are examples of decisions by West on whether to double for penalty.

WEST	NORTH	EAST	SOUTH
			1NT
?			

♠ A 9 5
♥ K Q J 10 9
♦ A K 8
♣ K 3

Double. Since there are four unbid suits when the opening bid is 1NT, using a double as takeout isn't very practical. To have support for all four suits, West would need a balanced hand and would be coming into an auction when South has already announced a strong balanced hand of 15-17 points. So, a double of 1NT is commonly treated as a penalty double in standard bidding. On this hand, a penalty double is a better choice than overcalling 2♥. West expects to defeat 1NT by at least one or two tricks after leading the ♥K. The penalty should be more than the score for making a partscore contract of 2♥.

WEST	NORTH	EAST	SOUTH
	2♠	PASS	4♠
?			

♠ K Q
♥ A K 6
♦ A 10 5 2
♣ A J 7 3

Double. North has opened with a weak two-bid and, based on West's high-card strength, South's jump to 4♠ is likely a preemptive raise, trying to make it difficult for East-West to enter the auction. Since North-South are at the game level, West's double is for penalty. West expects to take at least four or five tricks on defense against 4♠.

WEST	NORTH	EAST	SOUTH
1♥	1♠	2♥	2♠
?			

♠ K J 9 5
♥ A Q 8 6 3
♦ 5 2
♣ A 3

Pass. North-South's competitive bidding has prevented East-West from playing in 2♥ and West has good defensive prospects against the 2♠ contract but it would be risky to double. West has no guarantee the partnership can take enough tricks to defeat 2♠. Also, East-West are only in a partscore. If West doubles and North-South make 2♠, they will receive a game bonus instead of the partscore for 2♠.

SUMMARY

Responder's Action After an Overcall

When partner opens the bidding and the next player overcalls, responder can:

- Make the same response that would have been made without the overcall, if that is still possible.
- Make a suitable alternative response if the overcall has impacted responder's original choice.
- Use the new options available after the overcall:
  - Make a preemptive jump raise of opener's suit with four-card or longer support and a weak hand.
  - Use the cuebid of the opponents' suit to show support for opener's suit and at least invitational strength (11+).
  - Use the negative double to show support for the two unbid suits and enough strength to compete.

Responder's Action After a Takeout Double

When partner opens the bidding and the next player makes a takeout double, responder can:

- Redouble with 10 or more high-card points.
- Make a preemptive jump raise of opener's suit with four-card or longer support and a weak hand.
- Bid a new suit at the two level with fewer than 10 points.

Advancer's Actions in a Competitive Auction

When partner has overcalled or made a takeout double, advancer should strive to compete even if responder bids.

Opener's Actions in a Competitive Auction

Opener chooses a rebid based on responder's action. Opener can also use competitive calls such as the double.

The Penalty Double

A double is for penalty if:

- It is a double of an opponent's opening 1NT or 2NT bid.
- It is a double at the game level or higher.

Quiz – Part I

Neither side is vulnerable. North opens 1♦ and East overcalls 1♥. What call would South make with the following hands?

WEST	NORTH	EAST	SOUTH
	1♦	1♥	?

a) ♠ J 7 3
  ♥ 9 6 4
  ♦ 9 6 2
  ♣ K 8 7 5

b) ♠ K 10 9 7 4
  ♥ K 3
  ♦ 8 7 2
  ♣ J 8 4

c) ♠ Q 9 5
  ♥ K J 9
  ♦ J 8
  ♣ Q 10 7 4 2

d) ♠ 6 3
  ♥ 9 3
  ♦ A J 2
  ♣ A Q J 8 5 2

e) ♠ K 9 3
  ♥ Q 9 6 4
  ♦ K 8 4
  ♣ 10 9 5

f) ♠ Q 7 3
  ♥ A J 10
  ♦ K 9 5
  ♣ J 8 7 3

East-West are vulnerable; North-South are non vulnerable. North opens 1♥ and East overcalls 1♠. What call would South make with the following hands?

WEST	NORTH	EAST	SOUTH
	1♥	1♠	?

g) ♠ 7 3
  ♥ Q 8 5
  ♦ K 9 7 4
  ♣ Q 9 6 2

h) ♠ 4
  ♥ K J 8 4
  ♦ 10 8 6 5 4
  ♣ 6 4 2

i) ♠ 9 7 4
  ♥ Q 10 9 7 6 3
  ♦ 4
  ♣ Q 6 3

j) ♠ 8 5
  ♥ A Q 8 5
  ♦ K Q 7 4
  ♣ 10 9 2

k) ♠ 7 4 2
  ♥ A K J 6
  ♦ A 8 5
  ♣ K 6 4

l) ♠ 3 2
  ♥ K 10 2
  ♦ Q 7
  ♣ A J 10 8 6 3

Answers to Quiz – Part I

a) Pass. With only 4 high-card points, South was planning to pass if East passed. The overcall doesn't change South's decision.

b) 1♠. South would have responded 1♠ if East passed. South can still make the same call.

c) 1NT. With 9 high-card points plus 1 length point for the five-card club suit, South doesn't have enough strength to bid 2♣. Instead South responds 1NT.

d) 2♣. With 12 high-card points plus 2 length points for the six-card club suit, South has enough to bid a new suit at the two level.

e) 1NT. If East had not overcalled, South would have responded 1♥. After the overcall, 1NT is a reasonable alternative, showing 6-10 points with some strength in hearts.

f) 2NT. A jump to 2NT in response to 1♦ shows a balanced hand with enough strength to invite game, about 11–12 points.

g) 2♥. With three-card support for hearts and 7 high-card points plus 1 dummy point for the doubleton spade, South raises to 2♥.

h) 3♥. With four-card support for hearts and 4 high-card points plus 3 dummy points for the singleton spade, South can make a preemptive jump raise to 3♥ after East's overcall. If East had passed, a jump raise to 3♥ would be invitational, not weak.

i) 4♥. With a weak hand and six-card support for hearts, South can make a preemptive jump raise to 4♥ after the overcall.

j) 2♠. With four-card support and 12 points—11 high-card points plus 1 dummy point for the doubleton spade—South has enough to cuebid East's spades. Since a jump raise to 3♥ would be preemptive after the overcall,

k) 2♠. South's cuebid shows four-card or longer heart support and at least 11 points. On this hand, South has enough to continue to 4♥ even if North shows a minimum opening by rebidding 3♥. An immediate jump raise would be preemptive.

l) 2♣. Although South has three-card support for hearts, a cuebid tends to show four-card or longer support. Instead, South starts by bidding a new suit, planning to show the heart support later.

Quiz – Part II

Both sides are vulnerable. North opens 1♦ and East overcalls 1♠.
What call would South make as responder with each of the following hands?

WEST	NORTH	EAST	SOUTH
	1♦	1♠	?

a) ♠ 10 8 7
   ♥ Q J 7 5
   ♦ 6 2
   ♣ K Q 8 4

b) ♠ 6 5 4
   ♥ J 7 6 3
   ♦ 8 3
   ♣ Q 10 9 5

c) ♠ 5 3
   ♥ K 10 8 3
   ♦ A 9 5
   ♣ A Q 6 4

d) ♠ K J 9 8 7 4
   ♥ 8 4 3
   ♦ 6
   ♣ 8 5 2

e) ♠ 8 6 5
   ♥ A J 7 6
   ♦ 8 2
   ♣ A Q 10 7

f) ♠ 4 2
   ♥ Q 9 6 2
   ♦ J 5
   ♣ A J 8 7 3

Neither side is vulnerable. North opens 1♥ and East doubles. What
call would South make with the following hands?

WEST	NORTH	EAST	SOUTH
	1♥	DOUBLE	?

g) ♠ Q 8 5
   ♥ K J 5
   ♦ J 7 6 5 2
   ♣ 6 4

h) ♠ 5 3
   ♥ Q J 10 4
   ♦ 9 7
   ♣ Q J 8 7 5

i) ♠ 3
   ♥ K J 10 8 4
   ♦ J 9 8 7
   ♣ 9 8 2

j) ♠ K Q 10 8 5
   ♥ K 4
   ♦ 7 5 4 2
   ♣ 8 3

k) ♠ K J 7
   ♥ 6 2
   ♦ A Q 6 3
   ♣ J 9 8 3

l) ♠ 7 5
   ♥ 6 4
   ♦ Q 10 5
   ♣ K Q 10 9 8 4

Answers to Quiz – Part II

a)   Double. If East had passed, South would have responded 1♥. With only 8 high-card points, South isn't strong enough to bid a new suit at the two level but does have enough to compete. With four-card support for both unbid suits, South can make a negative double.

b)   Pass. Although South has four-card support for both unbid suits, the hand isn't strong enough to compete for the contract.

c)   Double. With 13 high-card points South has enough to take the partnership to game but starts with a negative double to show support for both unbid suits. If North bids 2♥, for example, South will jump to 4♥ to put the partnership in game in the eight-card fit.

d)   Pass. With length and strength in the overcalled suit, South should pass. A double would be negative, for takeout, not for penalty.

e)   Double. With support for both unbid suits and 11 high-card points, South starts with a negative double, planning to make a second bid to show a hand of invitational strength.

f)   Double. With 8 high-card points plus 1 length point, South has enough to compete by making a negative double after the 1♠ overcall. South isn't strong enough to bid 2♣, a new suit at the two level.

g)   2♥. With 7 high-card points plus 1 dummy point for the doubleton club, South has enough to raise opener's suit to the two level.

h)   3♥. With four-card support for hearts and 6 high-card points plus 1 dummy point for each doubleton, South could raise to 2♥ but a jump raise to 3♥ will likely be more effective in keeping East-West from finding their best contract. After the double, a jump raise is weak.

i)   4♥. With a weak hand and five-card support for North's hearts, South can make a preemptive jump raise to the four level. If North-South can't make 4♥, it's likely East-West can make a contract if left room to find their best spot.

j)   1♠. East's double doesn't prevent South from making the same response that South would have made if East had passed.

k)   Redouble. With 11 high-card points, South starts with a redouble to tell North the partnership has the majority of the strength.

l)   2♣. After the double, South's 2♣ call is not forcing and shows fewer than 10 high-card points. With 10 or more high-card points, South would start with a redouble.

Quiz – Part III

East-West are vulnerable and North-South are non vulnerable. What call would West make in each of the following auctions?

a)

WEST	NORTH	EAST	SOUTH
	1♣	DOUBLE	2♣
?			

♠ K J 8 4
♥ K 9 3
♦ J 5
♣ 9 7 4 2

b)

WEST	NORTH	EAST	SOUTH
1♦	1♠	DOUBLE	PASS
?			

♠ 7 4
♥ A 8 6 3
♦ K Q 9 8 5
♣ A 4

c)

WEST	NORTH	EAST	SOUTH
1♥	1♠	PASS	2♠
?			

♠ 4
♥ A K 7 6 4
♦ A K J
♣ K 10 9 2

d)

WEST	NORTH	EAST	SOUTH
1♥	1♠	2♥	4♠
?			

♠ K Q J
♥ A 9 8 5 3
♦ A 8 2
♣ A 7

Answers to Quiz – Part III

a) 2♠. East's double is for takeout and West is the advancer. When South bids, West is no longer obliged to bid. However, East is showing about 13 or more points and support for the unbid suits and West has 8 high-card points, enough to compete for the contract. East won't expect too much for West's 2♠ bid. With an invitational hand of about 9–11 points, West would jump to 3♠.

b) 2♥. East's double is negative, for takeout, showing enough strength to compete and support for the unbid suits, hearts and clubs. West can expect the partnership to have an eight-card fit in hearts.

c) Double. East hasn't shown any strength by passing after North's overcall but West has a strong opening bid—18 high-card points plus 1 length point for the five-card suit. West can double to show the extra strength. Since North-South are only in a partscore contract, West's double is for takeout, showing support for the unbid suits, diamonds and clubs, in addition to the five-card heart suit promised by the 1♥ opening bid.

d) Double. West has a strong hand and would have bid 4♥ if South had passed. South's jump to 4♠ is a preemptive raise of North's overcall, trying to make the auction difficult for East-West. West has enough to make a penalty double, expecting to defeat the 4♠ contract by at least two tricks, maybe more. West's double is for penalty, not takeout, since North-South have already reached the game level.

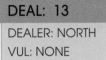

DEAL: 13

DEALER: NORTH

VUL: NONE

NORTH

WEST   EAST

SOUTH

NORTH
- ♠ 9 6
- ♥ Q J 10
- ♦ K J 9 5
- ♣ 9 7 6 2

WEST
- ♠ A Q 8 7 5
- ♥ 8 4 2
- ♦ 8 2
- ♣ K Q 4

EAST
- ♠ K 10 4
- ♥ 9 7 6 3
- ♦ Q 10 4
- ♣ A 8 5

SOUTH
- ♠ J 3 2
- ♥ A K 5
- ♦ A 7 6 3
- ♣ J 10 3

Suggested Bidding

WEST	NORTH	EAST	SOUTH
	Pass	Pass	1♦
1♠	2♦	2♠	Pass
Pass	Pass		

North has 7 high-card points and passes. East has 9 high-card points and passes. South has 13 high-card points, enough to open the bidding 1♦.

West has 11 high-card points plus 1 length point for the five-card suit. With a good suit, West has enough to overcall at the one level, 1♠.

North has support for opener's minor suit and can compete for the contract by raising to 2♦.

East also has support for partner's suit and enough strength to compete for the contract. East advances to 2♠.

South has a minimum opening bid and has nothing to add to the auction. South passes. Similarly, West doesn't have enough strength to bid again since East has shown only about 6-10 points in support of spades. West passes. North has nothing more to say and also passes, ending the auction.

The contract is 2♠ and West is the declarer.

Suggested Opening Lead

North leads the ♦5, low from three or more cards in the suit bid by the partnership. An alternative would be to lead the ♥Q, top of the solid sequence in hearts.

Declarer's Plan

West's goal is to take at least 8 tricks to make the 2♠ contract. West begins by counting the sure winners. There are five in spades if the five missing spades divide 3-2, as might be expected. There are also three in clubs. No more tricks are required.

```
┌── DECLARER'S PLAN—THE ABC'S ──┐
│ Declarer: West     Contract: 2♠ │
│                                 │
│ ASSESS THE SITUATION            │
│   Goal                    8     │
│   Sure Tricks             8     │
│   Extra Tricks Needed     0     │
│                                 │
│ BROWSE DECLARER'S CHECKLIST     │
│   Not applicable                │
│                                 │
│ CONSIDER THE ORDER              │
│   • Draw trumps first.          │
└─────────────────────────────────┘
```

The defenders will likely start by taking their two diamond winners and three heart winners. Whatever they lead next, declarer can win the trick. West's priority is to draw the defenders' trumps. This takes three rounds because the five missing spades are divided 3-2.

Once trumps are drawn, it is safe for declarer to take the club winners. On the actual lie, declarer could take the club winners before drawing trumps, but that's a risk declarer doesn't need to take.

Comments

On this deal, the overcall doesn't prevent North from raising South's diamonds, the same bid North would have made if West had passed. Similarly, North's raise doesn't prevent East from raising West's overcall. In a competitive auction, both sides try to buy the contract or push the other side too high.

If North-South were to bid 3♦, East-West will still score points by choosing to defend. They can get two spade tricks, a diamond, and three clubs on defense, defeating the contract two tricks. However, if East-West decide to push on to 3♠, now North-South will be the side to receive a positive score since 3♠ can be defeated.

In competitive auctions, both sides must use judgment to decide how to get the biggest plus score, or smallest minus score.

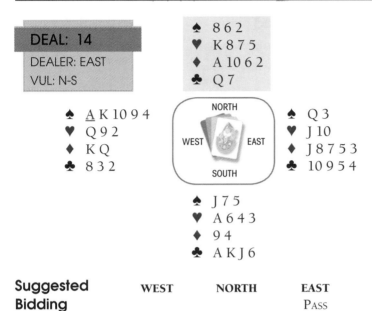

	DEAL: 14
	DEALER: EAST
	VUL: N-S

North:
♠ 8 6 2
♥ K 8 7 5
♦ A 10 6 2
♣ Q 7

West:
♠ A K 10 9 4
♥ Q 9 2
♦ K Q
♣ 8 3 2

East:
♠ Q 3
♥ J 10
♦ J 8 7 5 3
♣ 10 9 5 4

South:
♠ J 7 5
♥ A 6 4 3
♦ 9 4
♣ A K J 6

Suggested Bidding	**WEST**	**NORTH**	**EAST**	**SOUTH**
			PASS	1♣
	1♠	DOUBLE	PASS	2♥
	PASS	PASS	PASS	

East has 4 high-card points plus 1 length point for the five card suit. East passes.

South has 13 high-card points, enough to open the bidding. With no five-card major suit, South opens the minor suit, 1♣.

West has a good five-card suit and more than enough strength to overcall at the one level with 1♠.

North would have responded 1♦ or 1♥ if West had passed but, with only 9 high-card points, doesn't have enough strength to bid a new suit at the two level. A response of 2♥ would be forcing and the partnership might get too high. North does have enough strength to compete, however, and can use responder's double, the negative double, to show support for the unbid suits, hearts and diamonds.

East passes.

Since North has shown support for hearts and diamonds, South now bids 2♥, putting the partnership in its eight-card fit.

West has already described the hand and received no support from partner. West passes.

North also passes. South's bid at the cheapest available level has shown no extra strength, so the partnership likely belongs in partscore and has found its heart fit.

Suggested Opening Lead

West leads the ♠A, top of the touching cards in that suit. The ♦K would be another reasonable choice.

Declarer's Plan

South's goal is to take at least eight tricks to make the 2♥ contract. South begins by counting the sure winners: two hearts, one diamond, and four clubs for a total of seven tricks. One more trick is needed.

Moving to the second stage, South browses Declarer's Checklist. Declarer can develop an extra trick in hearts through length, provided the five missing hearts are divided 3-2.

```
┌─── DECLARER'S PLAN—THE ABC'S ───┐
│ Declarer: South    Contract: 2♥ │
│ ASSESS THE SITUATION            │
│   Goal                  8       │
│   Sure Tricks           7       │
│   Extra Tricks Needed   1       │
│ BROWSE DECLARER'S CHECKLIST     │
│   Promotion                     │
│   Length           1 in hearts  │
│   The Finesse                   │
│   Trumping in dummy             │
│ CONSIDER THE ORDER              │
│   • Draw trumps first.          │
│   • Play the high card from the │
│     short side first in clubs.  │
└─────────────────────────────────┘
```

West may start by leading the ♠A and ♠K, and then a third round which East can trump with the ♥10. Whichever suit East now leads, declarer can win. Before taking the club winners, declarer should first draw trumps. Declarer can take two tricks with the ♥A and ♥K and get a third trick in the suit after giving up a trick to West's ♥Q[44].

After regaining the lead, declarer can take the club winners, starting with the ♣Q, high card from the short side first.

Comments

By using the negative double, North and South find the eight-card heart fit despite West's interference. North-South can take eight tricks with hearts as trumps but only seven in a notrump contract.

---

[44] Declarer doesn't have to lead a third round of hearts on this deal. Declarer can simply leave the ♥Q outstanding and go about taking the club winners, letting West win the ♥Q whenever West wants.

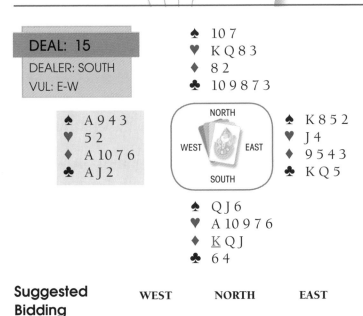

DEAL: 15

DEALER: SOUTH

VUL: E-W

NORTH
♠ 10 7
♥ K Q 8 3
♦ 8 2
♣ 10 9 8 7 3

WEST
♠ A 9 4 3
♥ 5 2
♦ A 10 7 6
♣ A J 2

EAST
♠ K 8 5 2
♥ J 4
♦ 9 5 4 3
♣ K Q 5

SOUTH
♠ Q J 6
♥ A 10 9 7 6
♦ K Q J
♣ 6 4

Suggested Bidding

WEST	NORTH	EAST	SOUTH
			1♥
DOUBLE	3♥	3♠(?)	PASS
PASS	PASS		

South, with 13 high-card points plus 1 point for the five-card heart suit, opens 1♥.

West has 13 high-card points and can add 1 dummy point for the doubleton heart. With support for the unbid suits, West's hand meets the requirements for a takeout double.

North, has 5 high-card points and, with four-card support for opener's suit, can add 1 dummy point for each doubleton. If West had passed, North would only raise to 2♥. West's double, however, has an effect on responder's priorities. With four-card support, North can make a preemptive (weak) jump raise to 3♥ to make it more challenging for East-West to find their best spot. After the double, the jump raise is no longer a limit raise showing about 11-12 points. With that much strength, North could redouble.

East, with 9 high-card points, would bid 2♠ if North passed or raised to 2♥. Over 3♥, East has a challenge. East doesn't want to let North-South win the contract with hearts as trumps but doesn't have quite enough strength to be comfortable competing to the three level. Nevertheless, East will probably make the slight overbid of 3♠.

South has nothing more to say since North has announced a weak hand. West also has nothing to add, having already made a takeout double. North has done enough and also passes, ending the auction.

Suggested Opening Lead

South leads the ♦K, top of the solid sequence. South might also consider leading the ♥A in the suit bid and raised by the partnership.

Declarer's Plan

East's goal is to take at least nine tricks. East can count on two tricks from the spade suit, one in diamonds, and three in clubs. Three more tricks are required.

With eight combined cards in spades, declarer can plan to gain a trick through length by losing one spade trick. Similarly, declarer can plan to get a trick through length in diamonds. In diamonds, declarer will have to lose two tricks. That's still not enough, but it's the best declarer can do.

```
┌─── DECLARER'S PLAN—THE ABC'S ───┐
 Declarer: East      Contract: 3♠

 ASSESS THE SITUATION
 Goal                    9
 Sure Tricks             6
 Extra Tricks Needed     3

 BROWSE DECLARER'S CHECKLIST
 Promotion
 Length               1 in spades
                      1 in diamonds
 The Finesse
 Trumping in dummy

 CONSIDER THE ORDER
  • Draw trumps first.
  • Take the losses early in diamonds
└─────────────────────────────────┘
```

After winning the ♦A, declarer can start by drawing trumps by taking the ♠A and ♠K. Declarer can leave South's ♠Q outstanding and go to work on diamonds. Declarer gives up a diamond trick to South. If the defenders take their two heart winners and lead a club, declarer wins and gives up one more trick in diamonds. This establishes a diamond trick which can be taken when declarer regains the lead.

Comments

North-South can't make 3♥ since the defenders have two spade tricks, a diamond, and two clubs. That's okay since East-West can make 2♠. Even better, the weak jump raise might push East-West too high.

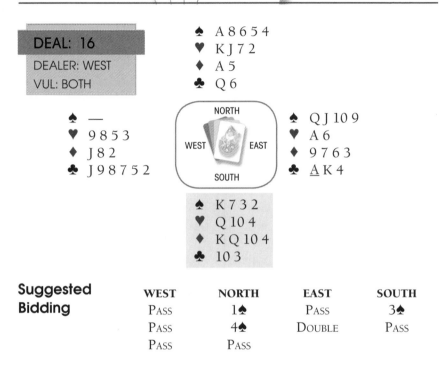

DEAL: 16

DEALER: WEST

VUL: BOTH

NORTH
♠ A 8 6 5 4
♥ K J 7 2
♦ A 5
♣ Q 6

WEST
♠ —
♥ 9 8 5 3
♦ J 8 2
♣ J 9 8 7 5 2

EAST
♠ Q J 10 9
♥ A 6
♦ 9 7 6 3
♣ A K 4

SOUTH
♠ K 7 3 2
♥ Q 10 4
♦ K Q 10 4
♣ 10 3

Suggested Bidding

WEST	NORTH	EAST	SOUTH
Pass	1♠	Pass	3♠
Pass	4♠	Double	Pass
Pass	Pass		

West passes with only 2 high-card points plus 2 length points for the six-card suit.

North has 14 high-card points plus 1 length point for the five-card suit. North opens 1♠, the five-card major suit.

East has 14 high-card points but doesn't have a five-card suit to overcall and doesn't have the support for the unbid suits for a takeout double. With no suitable way to enter the auction, East passes.

South has 10 high-card points and, with four-card support for North's major, can add 1 dummy point for the doubleton club. That's enough to make an invitational jump raise to 3♠.

West passes. North has more than a minimum opening, enough to accept responder's invitation and bid 4♠.

East, looking at two spade winners after the ♠A and ♠K have been played, the ♥A, and the ♣A-K, expects to defeat 4♠. East can make a penalty double. East's double is not for takeout. If East wanted to make a takeout double of spades, East would have doubled 1♠.

None of the other players has anything else to add, so the contract is 4♠ doubled with North as the declarer.

Suggested Opening Lead

East makes the opening lead against 4♠. East would lead the ♣A, top of the touching high cards in that suit.

Declarer's Plan

North is declarer and the goal is to take ten tricks. North counts two sure tricks in spades and three in diamonds. Five more tricks need to be developed.

North browses Declarer's Checklist. Three tricks can be promoted in hearts by driving out the ♥A. The spade suit may provide the additional tricks needed through length.

The number of tricks declarer will get from the spade

DECLARER'S PLAN—THE ABC'S

Declarer: North   Contract: 4♠ Dbl

ASSESS THE SITUATION
Goal	10
Sure Tricks	5
Extra Tricks Needed	5

BROWSE DECLARER'S CHECKLIST
Promotion	3 in hearts
Length	1–3 in spades
The Finesse	
Trumping in dummy	

CONSIDER THE ORDER
- Draw trumps.
- Take the losses early when promoting winners in the heart suit.

---

suit depends on how the four missing spades are divided in the defenders' hands. If they are 2-2, declarer can take all the tricks in the spade suit; if they are 3-1, declarer has to lose 1 trick but will get two tricks through length; if they are 4-0, declarer has to lose two tricks in the suit and will get only one trick through length.

On the actual deal, the spades divide badly and East gets two tricks in spades to go with the ♥A and ♣A-K. The contract is defeated two tricks. There is nothing declarer can do.

Comments

Even though the contract is defeated by two tricks, there is nothing wrong with the North-South bidding. If the missing trumps were divided 2-2, the game contract would make. The 4-0 division is unlucky and North-South are even unluckier if East makes use of the penalty double to increase the bonus for defeating the contract.

Practice is the best of all instructors.

—PUBLILIUS SYRUS, FIRST CENTURY B.C.

Additional
Practice Deals

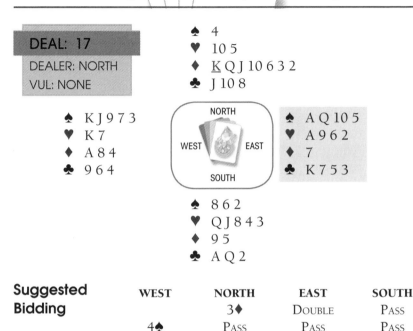

DEAL: 17			
DEALER: NORTH			
VUL: NONE			

NORTH
♠ 4
♥ 10 5
♦ K Q J 10 6 3 2
♣ J 10 8

WEST
♠ K J 9 7 3
♥ K 7
♦ A 8 4
♣ 9 6 4

EAST
♠ A Q 10 5
♥ A 9 6 2
♦ 7
♣ K 7 5 3

SOUTH
♠ 8 6 2
♥ Q J 8 4 3
♦ 9 5
♣ A Q 2

Suggested Bidding

WEST	NORTH	EAST	SOUTH
	3♦	DOUBLE	PASS
4♠	PASS	PASS	PASS

North has a good seven-card diamond suit and only 7 high-card points, ideal for a preemptive 3♦ opening bid. North and South are non vulnerable and North's hand is worth six playing tricks with diamonds as trumps. Even if the 3♦ bid is doubled and defeated three tricks, the penalty will be no more than 500 points (100 + 200 + 200).

East has a good hand for a takeout double even though the auction is at the three level. East has support for the unbid suits: spades, hearts, and clubs. There are 13 high-card points and 3 dummy points can be added for the singleton diamond, a total of 16 points.

South, as responder, doesn't have enough to compete further in the auction and passes.

West, the advancer, has 11 high-card points plus 1 length point for the five-card spade suit. East has promised 13 or more points, so West knows HOW HIGH the partnership belongs, game. West also knows WHERE the partnership belongs, spades. Putting it together, West jumps to 4♠. North, East, and South have nothing further to say, so West becomes declarer in a 4♠ contract.

Suggested Opening Lead

North leads the ♦K, top of the solid sequence, against West's 4♠.

Declarer's Plan

West's goal is to take ten tricks with spades as the trump suit. There are five sure spade tricks, two heart tricks, and the ♦A. That's a total of eight tricks; two more tricks must be developed.

West browses Declarer's Checklist. One possibility is the finesse in clubs. West could lead toward dummy's ♣K, hoping North holds the ♣A. This is unlikely to work, since North's opening bid showed few, if any,

> ┌─ DECLARER'S PLAN—THE ABC'S ─┐
>
> Declarer: West   Contract: 4♠
>
> **ASSESS THE SITUATION**
> Goal   10
> Sure Tricks   8
> Extra Tricks Needed   2
>
> **BROWSE DECLARER'S CHECKLIST**
> Promotion
> Length
> The Finesse   1 in clubs?
> Trumping in dummy   2 in diamonds
>
> **CONSIDER THE ORDER**
> • Keep enough trumps in the
>   dummy to trump two diamonds.

high cards outside diamonds. It is more likely South holds the ♣A. There is a second possibility. Since West has more diamonds than dummy, there is an opportunity to trump two diamonds in dummy.

In considering the order, declarer needs at least two spades in the dummy to trump diamonds. After winning the ♦A, declarer's best plan is to immediately lead another diamond and trump with East's ♠10[45]. Declarer then takes dummy's ♠A and plays the ♠5 to the ♠K. West leads the remaining diamond and trumps with dummy's ♠Q. Now declarer can lead a low heart from dummy to the ♥K and lead the ♠J to draw South's last trump. Declarer loses only three club tricks.

Comments

North's 3♦ opening bid carried little risk. On the lie of the cards, 3♦ can't be defeated since North can promote six diamond winners and take three club tricks with the help of finesses in clubs. The value of the preemptive bid is that it might keep East-West from reaching their 4♠ contract.

---

[45] Declarer trumps with a high spade so that South cannot overtrump with a higher spade if South has no diamonds remaining.

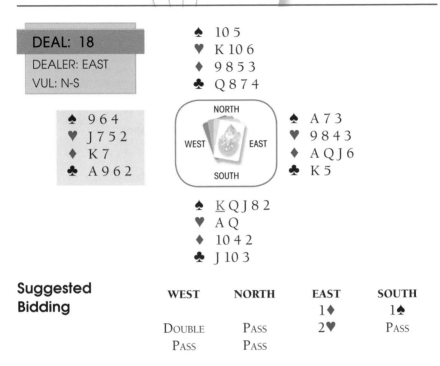

DEAL: 18

DEALER: EAST

VUL: N-S

NORTH
- ♠ 10 5
- ♥ K 10 6
- ♦ 9 8 5 3
- ♣ Q 8 7 4

WEST
- ♠ 9 6 4
- ♥ J 7 5 2
- ♦ K 7
- ♣ A 9 6 2

EAST
- ♠ A 7 3
- ♥ 9 8 4 3
- ♦ A Q J 6
- ♣ K 5

SOUTH
- ♠ K Q J 8 2
- ♥ A Q
- ♦ 10 4 2
- ♣ J 10 3

Suggested Bidding

WEST	NORTH	EAST	SOUTH
		1♦	1♠
DOUBLE	PASS	2♥	PASS
PASS	PASS		

East is the dealer and has 14 high-card points. With no five-card major suit, East opens 1♦, the longer minor suit.

South has 13 high-card points plus 1 length point for the five-card spade suit. South can compete for the contract with a 1♠ overcall.

West, as responder, would have bid 1♥ if South had passed. After the 1♠ overcall, West doesn't have enough strength to bid a new suit at the two level. With 8 high-card points and support for both unbid suits, hearts and clubs, however, West does have enough strength to want to compete for the contract. West can use responder's double—the negative double—to describe the hand.

North, as advancer, passes with only 5 high-card points.

East has to choose a rebid after responder's negative double, which is for takeout. With four hearts, even though they are all low cards, East bids 2♥, since West has shown support for hearts.

South, West, and North have nothing further to say and all pass. East becomes declarer in a 2♥ contract.

Suggested Opening Lead

South leads the ♠K, top of the solid sequence, against East's 2♥.

Declarer's Plan

East's goal is to take at least eight tricks. There is one sure spade trick, four diamond tricks, and two club tricks. One more trick is required.

East browses Declarer's Checklist. Even though the ♥A, ♥K, and ♥Q are missing, it may be possible to develop a heart trick through length with eight hearts between the combined hands. East has to hope the five missing hearts are divided 3-2.

Leading hearts also serves the

> ### DECLARER'S PLAN—THE ABC'S
>
> Declarer: East   Contract: 2♥
>
> **ASSESS THE SITUATION**
> | | |
> |---|---|
> | Goal | 8 |
> | Sure Tricks | 7 |
> | Extra Tricks Needed | 1 |
>
> **BROWSE DECLARER'S CHECKLIST**
> | | |
> |---|---|
> | Promotion | |
> | Length | 1 in hearts |
> | The Finesse | |
> | Trumping in dummy | |
>
> **CONSIDER THE ORDER**
> - Draw trumps.
> - Develop the extra heart trick early
> - High card from the short side first in diamonds.

purpose of drawing trumps. After winning the ♠A, declarer can immediately lead a heart to work on developing the extra trick early[46]. South can win the ♥Q and take two established spade winners, but no more. If South leads a diamond or a club, declarer can win and lead a second round of hearts. South can win the ♥A but, whatever South leads next, declarer can win and lead a third round of hearts to establish a winner after North takes the ♥K[47]. The defenders get only two spade tricks and three heart tricks.

When taking the diamonds, declarer starts with the ♦K, high card from the short side, and then plays the ♦7 over to the ♦A-Q-J.

Comments

East and West do well to find their 2♥ contract after South's 1♠ overcall by using the negative double. If North and South bid to 2♠, East-West can defeat that contract at least one trick.

[46] On this deal, declarer can actually do better by taking diamond winners early to discard spades from dummy, but drawing trumps works out well enough.

[47] Declarer doesn't have to lead a third round of hearts. Declarer can start taking winners in diamonds and clubs, letting North take a trick with the ♥K whenever North wants.

DEAL: 19
DEALER: SOUTH
VUL: E-W

♠ Q J 10 6
♥ 4
♦ 8 5 4
♣ 10 9 8 5 2

NORTH
WEST   EAST
SOUTH

West
♠ 9 2
♥ K Q 9 3
♦ A J 10
♣ A 6 4 3

East
♠ 8 4
♥ J 8 7 5 2
♦ K 7 2
♣ K Q 7

South
♠ A K 7 5 3
♥ A 10 6
♦ Q 9 6 3
♣ J

Suggested Bidding

WEST	NORTH	EAST	SOUTH
			1♠
DOUBLE	3♠	PASS(?)	PASS
PASS			

South is the dealer and values the hand as 15 points: 14 high-card points plus 1 length point for the five-card spade suit. With an unbalanced hand and a five-card major suit, South opens 1♠.

West can double with support for all three unbid suits and 14 high-card points plus 1 dummy point for the doubleton spade.

North has only 3 high-card points but, with four-card support for South's spades, can add three dummy points for the singleton heart, for a total of 6 points. If West had passed, North would raise to only 2♠ but, with an unbalanced hand and all the high-card points in partner's suit, North can make a preemptive raise to 3♠ over West's double. After the double, the jump raise is weak, not a limit raise.

East, as advancer, has 9 high-card points plus 1 length point for the five-card suit. If North had raised to 2♠, East has enough to compete to 3♥. When North jumps to 3♠, East doesn't have quite enough strength to bid 4♥. East passes.

South passes because North's raise is weak, not invitational.

Suggested Opening Lead

West leads the ♥K, top of the touching high cards, against 3♠.

Declarer's Plan

South's goal is to take nine tricks. There are five spade winners and the ♥A. Three more tricks are needed.

With two more hearts in declarer's hand than dummy, there is the opportunity to gain two tricks by trumping hearts in the dummy. With seven diamonds between the two hands, there is also the possibility to develop a diamond trick through length. This requires the missing diamonds to divide 3-3 which is a little against the odds, but a possibility[48].

In considering the order, declarer must make sure to leave two trumps in the dummy to ruff the hearts. Also, declarer should plan to lead diamonds early, before taking all the trump winners.

After winning the ♥A, declarer can lead the ♥6 and trump with one of dummy's spades. Declarer could then lead a diamond, planning to lose a trick in that suit. The defenders can take three diamond tricks and the ♣A, but declarer can eventually trump the ♥10 in dummy, draw trumps, and establish a diamond winner.

DECLARER'S PLAN—THE ABC'S

Declarer: South   Contract: 3♠

ASSESS THE SITUATION

Goal	9
Sure Tricks	6
Extra Tricks Needed	3

BROWSE DECLARER'S CHECKLIST

Promotion	
Length	1 in diamonds
The Finesse	
Trumping in dummy	2 in hearts

CONSIDER THE ORDER

- Keep enough trumps in the dummy to trump two hearts.
- Develop the extra diamond trick early.

Comments

North's jump to 3♠ may keep East-West from competing any further. If East-West compete to 4♥, North-South can defeat that contract[49].

---

[48] Declarer could hope to get a trick with the ♦Q by leading twice toward it, hoping East holds both the ♦A and ♦K. That's unlikely since West probably holds at least one high diamond for the takeout double. Another possibility is to try to trump the fourth round of diamonds in the dummy. That's unnecessary on the actual lie of the cards.

[49] If, for example, North leads the ♠Q against 4♥, South can overtake with the ♠K to win the trick and then lead the singleton ♣J. After winning a trick with the ♥A, South can lead a low spade to North's ♠J and North can lead a club for South to trump.

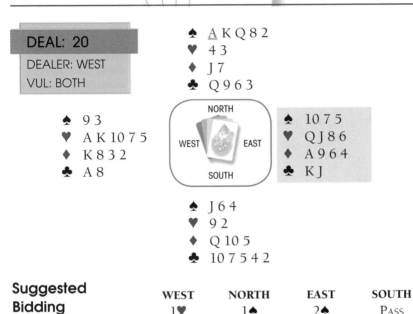

DEAL: 20

DEALER: WEST
VUL: BOTH

NORTH
♠ A K Q 8 2
♥ 4 3
♦ J 7
♣ Q 9 6 3

WEST
♠ 9 3
♥ A K 10 7 5
♦ K 8 3 2
♣ A 8

EAST
♠ 10 7 5
♥ Q J 8 6
♦ A 9 6 4
♣ K J

SOUTH
♠ J 6 4
♥ 9 2
♦ Q 10 5
♣ 10 7 5 4 2

Suggested Bidding

WEST	NORTH	EAST	SOUTH
1♥	1♠	2♠	Pass
4♥	Pass	Pass	Pass

West is the dealer with 14 high-card points plus 1 length point for the five-card heart suit. With an unbalanced hand, West opens 1♥.

North has 12 high-card points plus 1 length point for the five-card spade suit. North overcalls 1♠.

East has 11 high-card points and, with four-card support for West's hearts, can add 1 dummy point for the doubleton club. If North had passed, East would make a limit raise of 3♥, showing an invitational hand with about 11–12 points. After North's overcall, a jump to 3♥ would be preemptive, not a limit raise. To show the support and about 11 or more points, East cuebids 2♠, North's suit.

South has three-card support for spades but not enough strength to compete in the auction. South passes.

West has 15 points. That's enough to take the partnership to game after East cuebids to show support for hearts and 11 or more points. West jumps to 4♥.

North, East, and South all pass, ending the auction. West is declarer in 4♥.

Suggested Opening Lead

North leads the ♠A, top of the solid sequence, against West's 4♥ contract.

Declarer's Plan

The East hand comes down as the dummy and West makes a plan. West's goal is to take ten tricks.

West counts the sure tricks. There are five heart tricks, two diamonds, and two club tricks. One more trick is required.

West browses declarer's checklist. The diamond suit provides the opportunity for an extra trick through length. There are eight diamonds in the combined hands. If the five

┌─── DECLARER'S PLAN—THE ABC'S ───┐

Declarer: West   Contract: 4♥

ASSESS THE SITUATION
Goal   10
Sure Tricks   9
Extra Tricks Needed   1

BROWSE DECLARER'S CHECKLIST
Promotion
Length   1 in diamonds
The Finesse
Trumping in dummy

CONSIDER THE ORDER
- Draw trumps first.
- Develop the extra diamond trick early.

missing diamonds are divided 3-2, declarer can keep playing the suit until the defenders have no diamonds left. This establishes a third trick in the suit.

North will likely continue with the ♠K and ♠Q after winning the first trick with the ♠A. West can trump the third round of spades and then draw the defenders' trumps by playing the ♥A and ♥K. Declarer then takes two tricks with the ♦A and ♦K and plays a third round of diamonds, giving up a trick to the defenders. Declarer gives up the diamond trick early, while retaining winners in the other suits with which to regain the lead.

Comments

East and West reach their 4♥ contract despite North's 1♠ overcall. If East had jumped to 3♥ after the 1♠ overcall, West would pass, expecting East to hold a weak hand. When East cuebids 2♠, West jumps to 4♥ with some extra strength. If West rebids only 3♥, East might pass, assuming West held a minimum opening bid.

DEAL: 21	♠ 8 6	
DEALER: NORTH	♥ A K Q 10 3	
VUL: NONE	♦ A 6	
	♣ Q 9 6 5	

WEST	EAST
♠ 10 5 4 2	♠ A K Q 7
♥ J 7 6	♥ 9 5
♦ J 10 4 3	♦ K Q 7
♣ 7 3	♣ A J 4 2

SOUTH
♠ J 9 3
♥ 8 4 2
♦ 9 8 5 2
♣ K 10 8

Suggested Bidding

WEST	NORTH	EAST	SOUTH
	1♥	DOUBLE	PASS
1♠	PASS	3♠	PASS
PASS	PASS		

North has 15 high-card points plus 1 length point for the five-card heart suit. North opens 1♥, the five-card major suit.

East has 19 high-card points plus 1 dummy point for the doubleton heart. With support for all three unbid suits, East makes a takeout double.

South has only 4 high-card points and passes.

West has 2 high-card points but, as advancer, can't pass East's takeout double. West bids 1♠.

North doesn't have much extra for the opening bid and will probably pass since responder hasn't shown any strength. North might also choose to show another suit by bidding 2♣.

East has 20 points and excellent support for spades, but that isn't enough strength to commit the partnership to game. West has been forced to bid and might have no points at all. East issues a strong invitation by raising to 3♠, showing about 19–21 points.

After South passes, West also passes. West's 2 points are unlikely to be enough for game even though East has shown a strong hand.

North passes and the auction is over. West is declarer in a partscore contract of 3♠.

Suggested Opening Lead

North leads the ♥A, top of the solid sequence, against West's 3♠.

Declarer's Plan

West's goal is to take nine tricks with spades as the trump suit. There are three sure spade tricks and one sure club trick. Five more tricks are needed.

Declarer browses the checklist. If the five missing spades are divided 3-2, as might be expected, the spade suit will provide an extra trick through length. Since declarer has one more heart than dummy, declarer can gain a trick by trumping a heart in dummy. In diamonds, three tricks can be developed through promotion by driving out the ♦A.

DECLARER'S PLAN—THE ABC'S

Declarer: West   Contract: 3♠

ASSESS THE SITUATION

Goal	9
Sure Tricks	4
Extra Tricks Needed	5

BROWSE DECLARER'S CHECKLIST

Promotion	3 in diamonds
Length	1 in spades
The Finesse	
Trumping in dummy	1 in hearts

CONSIDER THE ORDER

- Keep enough trumps in the dummy to trump one heart.
- Draw trumps.
- High card from the short side whjen promoting diamond winners.

That's a lot of work to do, so declarer considers the order. Declarer wants to draw trumps before taking any promoted diamond winners. Declarer also wants to keep a spade in dummy to trump a heart.

Suppose North takes the ♥A and ♥K and leads a club. Declarer wins the ♣A and draws the defenders trumps with the ♠A–K–Q. Now declarer can lead the ♦K, high card from the short side. North can win the ♦A and the defenders can take a club trick, but that's all. If they lead another club, West trumps. West can trump a heart in dummy and take the ♦Q and two more tricks with the ♦J-10.

Comments

Despite holding 20 points, East must not take the partnership too high. All East-West can make is a partscore contract in spades.

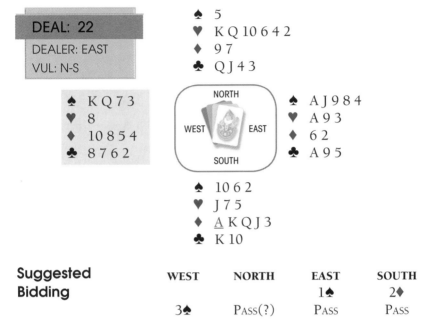

DEAL: 22

DEALER: EAST
VUL: N-S

NORTH
♠ 5
♥ K Q 10 6 4 2
♦ 9 7
♣ Q J 4 3

WEST
♠ K Q 7 3
♥ 8
♦ 10 8 5 4
♣ 8 7 6 2

EAST
♠ A J 9 8 4
♥ A 9 3
♦ 6 2
♣ A 9 5

SOUTH
♠ 10 6 2
♥ J 7 5
♦ A K Q J 3
♣ K 10

Suggested
Bidding

WEST	NORTH	EAST	SOUTH
		1♠	2♦
3♠	PASS(?)	PASS	PASS

East is the dealer and has 13 high-card points plus 1 length point for the five-card spade suit. East opens 1♠, the five-card major suit.

South has 14 high-card points and 1 length point for the five-card diamond suit. With a good diamond suit, South overcalls 2♦.

West has 5 high-card points but, with four-card support for East's spades, can add 3 dummy points for the singleton heart. If South had passed, West would raise to 2♠, showing 6-9 points. Once the auction becomes competitive, taking bidding room away from the opponents becomes important. With four-card support, an unbalanced hand, and a concentration of high cards in spades, West makes a preemptive jump raise to 3♠.

North, as advancer, might have bid 2♥ if West had passed and might even compete with 3♥ if West raised only to 2♠. After West raises to 3♠, North will probably keep out of the auction and pass.

East passes. West's jump to 3♠ has not promised much strength.

South passes and East becomes declarer in a partscore contract of 3♠.

Suggested Opening Lead

South leads the ♦A, top of the solid sequence, against East's 3♠.

Declarer's Plan

East's goal is to take at least nine tricks. There are five sure trick in spades, the ♥A, and ♣A. Two more tricks are required.

East browses Declarer's Checklist for ways to develop the extra tricks. Declarer has two more hearts than there are in the dummy. This provides the opportunity to gain two tricks by trumping hearts in the dummy.

In considering the order,

```
┌─── DECLARER'S PLAN—THE ABC'S ───┐
  Declarer: East      Contract: 3♠

  ASSESS THE SITUATION
    Goal                     9
    Sure Tricks              7
    Extra Tricks Needed      2

  BROWSE DECLARER'S CHECKLIST
    Promotion
    Length
    The Finesse
    Trumping in dummy   2 in hearts

  CONSIDER THE ORDER
    • Keep enough trumps in the
      dummy to trump two hearts.
└─────────────────────────────────┘
```

declarer must be careful to keep at least two trumps in the dummy with which to ruff the hearts. Declarer may have to delay drawing all the trumps until the hearts are ruffed.

Suppose South takes two tricks with the ♦A and ♦K and then leads the ♦Q. East trumps the third round and can immediately play the ♥A and lead the ♥3 and trump it in dummy. The declarer can take the ♠K and lead a spade to the ♠A. Now declarer leads the ♥9 and trumps in the dummy. Since there are no spades left in dummy to draw the last trump, a low club is led to declarer's ♣A. Declarer can then draw South's remaining spade by playing the ♠J.

Comments

North-South can actually make 4♥ if they can reach that contract. As declarer in 4♥, North would lose only one spade trick, the ♥A, and ♣A. West's preemptive jump raise to 3♠ is effective in making it difficult for North-South to find their best contract.

If North and South do bid 4♥, East might choose to bid 4♠ in the knowledge that West has a weak hand but four-card trump support. Since 4♠ is only defeated one trick, it is a good sacrifice against North-South's game contract.

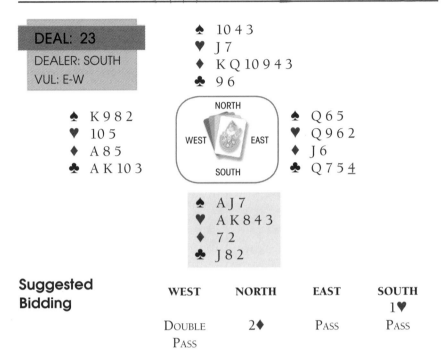

DEAL: 23

DEALER: SOUTH

VUL: E-W

NORTH

♠ 10 4 3
♥ J 7
♦ K Q 10 9 4 3
♣ 9 6

WEST

♠ K 9 8 2
♥ 10 5
♦ A 8 5
♣ A K 10 3

EAST

♠ Q 6 5
♥ Q 9 6 2
♦ J 6
♣ Q 7 5 4

SOUTH

♠ A J 7
♥ A K 8 4 3
♦ 7 2
♣ J 8 2

Suggested Bidding

WEST	NORTH	EAST	SOUTH
			1♥
DOUBLE	2♦	PASS	PASS
PASS			

South values the hand as 14 points: 13 high-card points plus 1 length point for the five-card heart suit. South opens 1♥, the five-card major.

West makes a takeout double with 14 high-card points plus 1 dummy point for the doubleton heart and support for the unbid suits.

North has 6 high-card points plus 2 length points for the six-card suit. If West had passed, North would not have enough strength to bid a new suit at the two level and would respond 1NT. After West's takeout double, North can bid 2♦. A new suit at the two level is not forcing after the double. With 10 or more points, North would redouble.

East, as advancer, would have to bid if North passed. When North bids 2♦, East no longer has to bid. With only 7 high-card points, East doesn't have enough strength to compete to 3♣. East passes.

South has nothing extra for the opening bid and North's 2♦ is not forcing, so South can pass.

West, with minimum values for the takeout double, passes and the auction is over. North is declarer in 2♦.

Suggested Opening Lead

East doesn't have a clear cut choice of opening lead against North's 2♦ contract. East might choose the ♣4, fourth highest from a suit with no touching high cards.

Declarer's Plan

North's goal is to take eight tricks. There is one sure spade trick and there are two sure heart tricks. Five more tricks are needed.

Declarer browses the checklist. Declarer can plan to develop five winners in the diamond suit through a combination of the finesse and length.

Suppose West wins the first two tricks with the ♣A-K and

DECLARER'S PLAN—THE ABC'S		
Declarer: North	Contract: 2♦	
ASSESS THE SITUATION		
Goal		8
Sure Tricks		3
Extra Tricks Needed		5
BROWSE DECLARER'S CHECKLIST		
Promotion		
Length		4 in diamonds
The Finesse		1 in diamonds
Trumping in dummy		
CONSIDER THE ORDER		
• Be in the right hand to lead toward the ♦K and ♦Q.		

then leads another club. North can trump the third round of clubs and should now go after diamonds. On the actual deal, declarer can lead the ♦K to drive out the ♦A and will then take five diamond tricks because the ♦J falls under the ♦Q.

A better approach is to lead toward the cards North hopes will take tricks, the ♦K and ♦Q, hoping West holds the ♦A. North plays the ♥7 to dummy's ♥K and leads a diamond toward the ♦K-Q. If West plays the ♦A, North can play low and later use the ♦K and ♦Q to draw the remaining trumps. If West plays low, North wins with the ♦Q (or ♦K). North then leads the ♥J to dummy's ♥A to lead another diamond. If West plays the ♦A, North plays low; if West plays low, North wins the ♦K. By playing diamonds in this fashion, declarer doesn't have to rely on the ♦J falling on the second round.

Comments

North and South do well to get to a partscore of 2♦ after West's takeout double. That's their best contract. If North were to bid 1NT instead of 2♦, for example, that contract can be defeated.

DEAL: 24

DEALER: WEST

VUL: BOTH

♠ Q 7 6 2
♥ 6 4 2
♦ Q 5 4
♣ 7 5 2

♠ 10 4
♥ A J 10 8
♦ 10 9 7
♣ K Q 10 6

NORTH

WEST   EAST

SOUTH

♠ A K J 9 5
♥ 9 3
♦ K J 6 2
♣ 8 4

♠ 8 3
♥ K Q 7 5
♦ A 8 3
♣ A J 9 3

Suggested Bidding

WEST	NORTH	EAST	SOUTH
PASS	PASS	1♠	DOUBLE
REDOUBLE	PASS	PASS	2♣/2♥
DOUBLE	PASS	PASS	PASS

West is the dealer and, with only 10 high-card points, passes.

North has 4 high-card points and also passes.

East, with 12 high-card points plus 1 length point for the five-card spade suit, opens 1♠.

South makes a takeout double with support for the unbid suits and 14 high-card points plus 1 dummy point for the doubleton spade.

West shows 10 or more high-card points by redoubling. The redouble sends the message that East-West has the majority of strength.

If West had passed, North would have to bid something. After the redouble, North can pass with no real preference for any of the unbid suits.

East should also pass, waiting to see how the auction will develop.

South doesn't want to defend 1♠ redoubled[50], so South bids one of the four-card suits, either 2♣ or 2♥.

---

[50] The trick score for making 1♠ would be multiplied by four, making it enough for a game bonus. Also, overtricks would be worth 400 points each (see Appendix 2).

West, having redoubled, can now make a penalty double of whichever suit South chooses. The penalty should be more than any score East-West would receive for making a partscore or game contract. West's penalty double should end the auction.

Suggested Opening Lead

West leads the ♠10, top of the doubleton in partner's suit.

Declarer's Plan

In a contract of 2♣ doubled (or 2♥ doubled), South's goal is to take eight tricks. South counts the sure tricks. There is one in diamonds and one in clubs. Six more tricks are needed.

South browses Declarer's Checklist. One winner can be promoted in the heart suit, but it's difficult to see where additional tricks will come from. South could try leading toward

DECLARER'S PLAN—THE ABC'S		
Declarer: South	Contract: 2♣ Dbl	
ASSESS THE SITUATION		
Goal		8
Sure Tricks		2
Extra Tricks Needed		6
BROWSE DECLARER'S CHECKLIST		
Promotion	1 in hearts	
Length	1 in hearts or clubs?	
The Finesse	1 in diamonds?	
Trumping in dummy		
CONSIDER THE ORDER		
• Take the tricks and run!		

dummy's ♦Q, hoping West has the ♦K, but that doesn't work. South could hope the missing clubs or hearts are divided 3-3 and an extra trick can be developed through length but both suits divide 4-2.

On a deal like this, South will have difficulty taking more than three or four tricks without some help from the defense. West might lead the ♥A, for example, establishing two tricks for declarer. South will have to settle for whatever tricks are available.

Comments

This deal illustrates the potential danger in competing. There is nothing wrong with the takeout double but, when East-West hold the balance of strength, it's possible to run into a large penalty.

To get a large penalty, East and West have to make effective use of the redouble. That takes some cooperation and this deal shows how it can be done.

	♠ 7 5 3 2
DEAL: 25	♥ K 10 2
DEALER:NORTH	♦ J 5
VUL: NONE	♣ Q 7 5 2

♠ Q 4	NORTH	♠ A K J 10 8
♥ 6 4 3	WEST EAST	♥ 7 5
♦ 10 8 7 3 2		♦ Q 9
♣ 10 8 4	SOUTH	♣ K J 9 3

| ♠ 9 6 |
| ♥ A Q J 9 8 |
| ♦ A K 6 4 |
| ♣ A 6 |

**Suggested
Bidding**

WEST	NORTH	EAST	SOUTH
	PASS	1♠	DOUBLE
PASS	2♣	PASS	2♥
PASS	3♥	PASS	4♥
PASS	PASS	PASS	

North has 6 high-card points and passes.

East has 14 high-card points plus 1 length point for the five-card spade suit. With an unbalanced hand, East opens 1♠.

South has 18 high-card points plus 1 length point for the five-card suit, for a total of 19 points. That's too much for a simple overcall of 2♥. Instead of overcalling, South starts with a takeout double.

West passes with only 2 high-card points and 1 length point.

North, the advancer, assumes South has a standard takeout double. With only 6 high-card points, North bids 2♣, bidding the four-card suit at the cheapest level.

East, having opened, has nothing more to say and passes.

South now shows the true nature of the hand by bidding 2♥. The double followed by the bid of new suit shows a hand too strong to overcall, about 18 or more points.

After West passes, North with support for hearts and knowing South has a strong hand, raises to 3♥.

After East passes, South takes the partnership to game in 4♥. Everyone passes and the auction is over.

Suggested Opening Lead

West leads the ♠Q, top of the doubleton in partner's suit.

Declarer's Plan

South's goal is to take ten tricks with hearts as the trump suit. There are five hearts, two diamonds, and one club trick. Two more tricks need to be developed.

South browses Declarer's Checklist. With more diamonds in declarer's hand than dummy, there is the opportunity to gain two tricks by trumping diamonds in dummy.

In considering the order, declarer wants to keep enough trumps in the dummy to ruff

┌─ **DECLARER'S PLAN—THE ABC'S** ─┐

Declarer: South   Contract: 4♥

ASSESS THE SITUATION
Goal	10
Sure Tricks	8
Extra Tricks Needed	2

BROWSE DECLARER'S CHECKLIST
Promotion
Length
The Finesse
Trumping in dummy 2 in diamonds

CONSIDER THE ORDER
- Keep enough hearts in dummy to trump two diamonds.
- Trump high to avoid being over-trumped.

the diamonds. That means declarer has to delay drawing trumps.

Suppose the defenders win the first two spade tricks and East leads a third round. South trumps with the ♥8. Declarer can afford to take one round of trumps by playing the ♥A, but that's all for now. Declarer next takes the ♦A-K and leads a third round and trumps with dummy's ♥10. Even though East has no more diamonds, East has no heart higher than the ♥10 with which to overruff.

Declarer can now play a low club from dummy to the ♣A and lead a fourth round of diamonds to trump with dummy's ♥K. Declarer still has two high hearts left to make ten tricks.

Comments

If South were to overcall 2♥, North-South might miss a game contract if North doesn't raise. To show a hand too strong for a simple overcall, South doubles first and then bids the long suit.

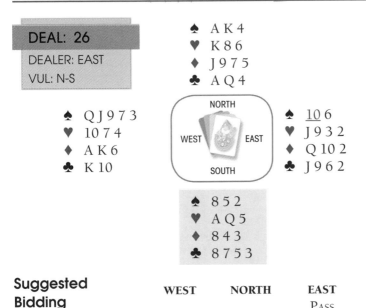

DEAL: 26

DEALER: EAST
VUL: N-S

NORTH
- ♠ A K 4
- ♥ K 8 6
- ♦ J 9 7 5
- ♣ A Q 4

WEST
- ♠ Q J 9 7 3
- ♥ 10 7 4
- ♦ A K 6
- ♣ K 10

EAST
- ♠ 10 6
- ♥ J 9 3 2
- ♦ Q 10 2
- ♣ J 9 6 2

SOUTH
- ♠ 8 5 2
- ♥ A Q 5
- ♦ 8 4 3
- ♣ 8 7 5 3

Suggested Bidding

WEST	NORTH	EAST	SOUTH
		Pass	Pass
1♠	1NT	Pass	Pass
Pass			

East has 4 high-card points and passes. South has 6 high-card points and passes.

West, with 13 high-card points plus 1 length point for the five-card spade suit, opens 1♠.

North has a balanced hand with 17 high-card points. If West had passed, North would open 1NT. After West's 1♠ opening, North, with some strength in spades, can still show the same type of hand by overcalling 1NT.

East doesn't have enough for a response to 1♠ and passes.

South doesn't have enough to take the partnership any higher after North's 1NT overcall.

West also passes, ending the auction. North becomes declarer in a contract of 1NT.

Suggested Opening Lead

East leads the ♠10, top of the doubleton in partner's suit.

Declarer's Plan

South puts down the dummy and North makes a plan. North's goal is to take at least seven tricks. There are two sure tricks in spades, three in hearts, and one in clubs. One more trick is required.

North browses Declarer's Checklist. The club suit provides the possibility of an extra trick through a finesse. North can hope that West holds the ♣K and plan to take two tricks with the ♣A-Q rather than one.

DECLARER'S PLAN—THE ABC'S

Declarer: North   Contract: 1NT

ASSESS THE SITUATION

Goal	7
Sure Tricks	6
Extra Tricks Needed	1

BROWSE DECLARER'S CHECKLIST

Promotion	
Length	
The Finesse	1 in clubs
Trumping in dummy	

CONSIDER THE ORDER

- Be in the right place at the right time to lead toward the ♣Q.

To take a finesse in clubs, declarer must be in the right place at the right time to lead toward the ♣Q. After winning a trick with the ♠K, declarer can play a low heart to South's ♥Q or ♥A. Now declarer is in the right hand to try the club finesse.

Declarer leads a low club from dummy and, when West plays the ♣10, declarer finesses the ♣Q. Since East doesn't hold the ♣K, the ♣Q wins and declarer has the extra trick needed to make the contract. It wouldn't help West to play the ♣K when a low club is led from dummy, North would win the ♣A and have the ♣Q as a second trick in the suit. After the club finesse works, declarer can take the remaining winners to make the contract.

Comments

A 1NT overcall is similar to a 1NT opening bid. Advancer bids in the same way as when responding to a 1NT opening. Advancer decides HOW HIGH and WHERE the partnership belongs.

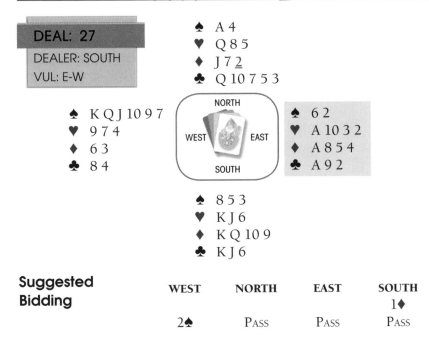

DEAL: 27	♠ A 4
DEALER: SOUTH	♥ Q 8 5
VUL: E-W	♦ J 7 2
	♣ Q 10 7 5 3

WEST
♠ K Q J 10 9 7
♥ 9 7 4
♦ 6 3
♣ 8 4

EAST
♠ 6 2
♥ A 10 3 2
♦ A 8 5 4
♣ A 9 2

SOUTH
♠ 8 5 3
♥ K J 6
♦ K Q 10 9
♣ K J 6

Suggested Bidding

WEST	NORTH	EAST	SOUTH
			1♦
2♠	PASS	PASS	PASS

South is the dealer and has 13 high-card points. With no five-card major suit, South opens 1♦, the longer minor suit.

West has only 6 high-card points but a good six-card suit. With five playing tricks, West can make a weak jump overcall of 2♠ to both describe the hand and take away bidding room from North-South.

North has 9 high-card points plus 1 length point for the five-card suit but not enough strength to bid a new suit at the three level. The hand is also unsuitable for a negative double because North doesn't have four-card support for hearts. North passes[51].

East has 12 high-card points, but not enough to bid anything after West's weak jump overcall. East can provide 3 tricks, but that won't be enough for the partnership to make 4♠ since West is showing only 5 or 6 playing tricks. East passes.

South has nothing more to say and also passes, ending the auction.

---

[51] North might bid 2NT, although this tends to show about 11–12 points.

Suggested Opening Lead

North might choose the ♦2, low from three or more cards in partner's suit, against East's 2♠ contract.

Declarer's Plan

After North's ♦2 lead, East puts down the dummy and West's goal is to take eight tricks with spades as trumps. There is one sure trick in hearts, one in diamonds, and one in clubs. Five more tricks are needed.

Declarer browses the checklist. Declarer can plan to develop five winners in the spade suit through promotion.

After winning the first trick, declarer can immediately lead a

```
┌─ DECLARER'S PLAN—THE ABC'S ─┐
  Declarer: West    Contract: 2♠

  ASSESS THE SITUATION
  Goal                    8
  Sure Tricks             3
  Extra Tricks Needed     5

  BROWSE DECLARER'S CHECKLIST
  Promotion          5 in spades
  Length
  The Finesse
  Trumping in dummy

  CONSIDER THE ORDER
  • Draw trumps first.
  • Develop the extra spade tricks
    early.
└──────────────────────────────┘
```

spade, planning to drive out the defenders' ♠A. This serves two purposes: promoting winners in the spade suit and drawing trumps.

After North wins the ♠A, the defenders can take a diamond trick but whatever they lead next can be won by declarer. Declarer draws the remaining trumps and takes five spade tricks to go with the ♥A, ♦A, and ♣A to make the contract.

Comments

West's jump overcall is a little risky since East-West is vulnerable and North-South is not. With such a solid spade suit, however, it's unlikely that North-South will make a penalty double. The value of the preemptive jump overcall is that it may keep North-South out of the auction. North-South can make 2NT or 3♣ but it isn't easy to get there after West's interference.

East should not consider playing in notrump. If the defenders hold up taking the ♠A for one round, East will get only one trick from the spade suit to go with the three aces.

DEAL: 28			
DEALER: WEST			
VUL: BOTH			

NORTH
- ♠ 4
- ♥ 7 6 3
- ♦ K Q J 10 9 8 4
- ♣ 8 3

WEST
- ♠ K 6
- ♥ A K 8
- ♦ 7 5 2
- ♣ Q J 10 9 7

EAST
- ♠ A J 8 5 2
- ♥ 9 5 4
- ♦ A 3
- ♣ K 6 4

SOUTH
- ♠ Q 10 9 7 3
- ♥ Q J 10 2
- ♦ 6
- ♣ A 5 2

Suggested Bidding

WEST	NORTH	EAST	SOUTH
1♣	3♦	3♠	PASS
4♠(?)	PASS	PASS	PASS

West is the dealer and has 14 valuation points: 13 high-card points plus 1 length point for the five-card club suit. West opens 1♣.

North has only 6 high-card points but an excellent seven-card suit. North can make a weak jump overcall of 3♦[52].

East has 12 high-card points plus 1 length point for the five-card spade suit. East would have responded 1♠ if North had passed. The 3♦ overcall makes East's call more challenging. East will probably choose to bid 3♠, showing the spade suit.

South has 9 high-card points plus 1 length point for the five-card spade suit. With no fit for partner's diamond suit, South passes.

West is awkwardly placed over East's forcing 3♠ bid. West doesn't have strength in diamonds, so 3NT is unattractive. It isn't particularly attractive to rebid the five-card club suit at the four level. West might choose to raise partner's spades to game, even with only two spades. East has at least a five-card suit and perhaps six or more.

[52] North-South are vulnerable so, with six playing tricks, North might choose to jump to only 2♦, following the Guideline of 500. A jump to 3♦ is likely to be more effective in taking away bidding room from the opponents and, with East-West also being vulnerable, is not too risky.

Suggested Opening Lead

South leads the ♦6, partner's suit, against East's 4♠ contract.

Declarer's Plan

East's goal is to take ten tricks with spades as trumps. There are two spade tricks, two hearts, and one diamond. Five more trick are needed.

East browses Declarer's Checklist. East can plan to promote extra tricks in clubs. However, the key will be to avoid losing three tricks in the trump suit. East can hope that North holds the ♠Q and may get an extra trick by finessing

> ### DECLARER'S PLAN—THE ABC'S
>
> Declarer: East   Contract: 4♠
>
> **A**SSESS THE SITUATION
>
> | Goal | 10 |
> |---|---|
> | Sure Tricks | 5 |
> | Extra Tricks Needed | 5 |
>
> **B**ROWSE DECLARER'S CHECKLIST
>
> | Promotion | 4 in clubs |
> |---|---|
> | Length | 2 in spades? |
> | The Finesse | 1 in spades? |
> | Trumping in dummy | |
>
> **C**ONSIDER THE ORDER
>
> - Draw trumps.
> - Play the high card from the short side first when promoting clubs.

the ♠J. East may also get extra spade tricks through length, if the missing spades divide 3-3 or 4-2.

North's 3♦ bid, showing a long diamond suit and a weak hand makes it unlikely North holds the ♠Q or that the six missing spades will divide favorably. On the actual layout, South has three spade winners to go with the ♣A, enough to defeat the contract. Declarer will be able to promote winners in dummy's club suit and use them to discard a heart and a diamond, but that's the best East can do.

Comments

This deal illustrates the effectiveness of the weak jump overcall. A jump to 3♦ by North is more effective than a jump to 2♦ and could push East-West into a poor contract. East-West can make 3NT, but it is difficult to get there after North's interference.

If East-West were to double 3♦, they would defeat the contract only one trick. North can promote six diamond tricks and a heart trick to go along with the ♣A.

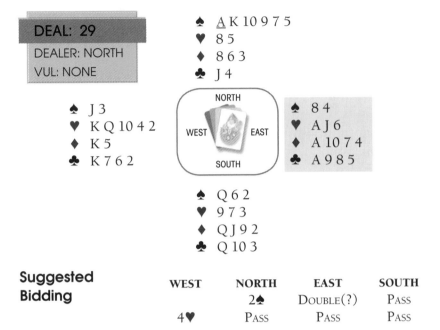

	DEAL: 29		♠ A K 10 9 7 5
			♥ 8 5
	DEALER: NORTH		♦ 8 6 3
	VUL: NONE		♣ J 4

♠ J 3
♥ K Q 10 4 2
♦ K 5
♣ K 7 6 2

♠ 8 4
♥ A J 6
♦ A 10 7 4
♣ A 9 8 5

♠ Q 6 2
♥ 9 7 3
♦ Q J 9 2
♣ Q 10 3

Suggested Bidding

WEST	NORTH	EAST	SOUTH
	2♠	DOUBLE(?)	PASS
4♥	PASS	PASS	PASS

North has 8 high-card points plus 2 length points for the six-card spade suit. With a good six-card suit and less than the values for an opening bid at the one level, North opens with a weak 2♠ bid.

East has 13 high-card points and support for the unbid suits. East can add 1 dummy point for the doubleton spade. Although the auction is already at the two-level and East has only three-card support for hearts, East will probably choose to make a takeout double. North's preemptive opening has created a challenge for East and West and, if they don't take some risk, they may be effectively shut out of the auction.

South, with three-card support for spades, might choose to further North's preemptive action by raising to 3♠. With a balanced hand and only queens and jacks, however, South might prefer to pass.

West, as advancer, has 12 high-card points plus 1 length point for the five-card heart suit. East has promised at least 13 points with the takeout double—perhaps a bit more since the double was at the two level. That's enough for West to know How High. The partnership has enough combined strength for game. West also knows WHERE. West can bid 4♥, with the knowledge that East's double has shown support for hearts.

Suggested Opening Lead

North leads the ♠A, top of the touching high cards, against 4♥.

Declarer's Plan

West's goal is to take ten tricks with hearts as the trump suit.

There are five heart tricks, two diamond tricks, and two club tricks. One more trick need to be developed.

East browses Declarer's Checklist. There are eight clubs between the combined hands, so the club suit might provide an extra trick through length if the five missing clubs are divided 3-2.

DECLARER'S PLAN—THE ABC'S

Declarer: West   Contract: 4♥

ASSESS THE SITUATION
Goal	10
Sure Tricks	9
Extra Tricks Needed	1

BROWSE DECLARER'S CHECKLIST
Promotion	
Length	1 in clubs
The Finesse	
Trumping in dummy	

CONSIDER THE ORDER
- Draw trumps first.
- Take the loss early in clubs.

The defenders may take the first two spade tricks and lead a diamond. Declarer wins, and the first priority is to draw the defenders' trumps. Declarer then goes about establishing the extra trick in clubs while still holding winners in the other suits to regain the lead.

Declarer takes the ♣A and ♣K. When both defenders follow suit, there is only one club outstanding. Declarer leads another club, giving up a trick to South's ♣Q. Declarer now has the rest of the tricks since declarer's remaining club is a winner.

Comments

North's weak 2♠ opening presents a challenge to East-West. If they don't enter the auction, North will buy the contract in 2♠ and take at least six tricks, perhaps seven if the defenders don't trump one of the potential diamond winners. Down two, even doubled, would be a good result for North-South since East-West can make a game contract.

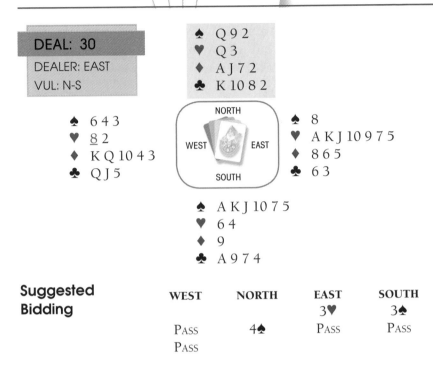

DEAL: 30

DEALER: EAST

VUL: N-S

NORTH
♠ Q 9 2
♥ Q 3
♦ A J 7 2
♣ K 10 8 2

WEST
♠ 6 4 3
♥ 8 2
♦ K Q 10 4 3
♣ Q J 5

EAST
♠ 8
♥ A K J 10 9 7 5
♦ 8 6 5
♣ 6 3

SOUTH
♠ A K J 10 7 5
♥ 6 4
♦ 9
♣ A 9 7 4

Suggested Bidding

WEST	NORTH	EAST	SOUTH
		3♥	3♠
PASS	4♠	PASS	PASS
PASS			

East is the dealer. Although there are only 8 high-card points, East has an excellent seven-card heart suit. Without enough strength to open 1♥, East opens with a preemptive 3♥ bid. East's heart suit is worth about seven playing tricks.

South has 12 high-card points plus 2 length points for the six-card spade suit. South would be comfortable opening the bidding 1♠, but is faced with a more challenging decision when East opens 3♥. With the good six-card suit, South has enough to risk an overcall at the three level.

West has only two-card support for hearts and can only provide about one playing trick, so West will probably choose to pass.

North has support for South's spades and 12 high-card points. That's enough to take the partnership to game in 4♠. North can expect South to hold at least an opening bid for the overcall at the three level.

East, South, and West will likely all pass and South will be declarer in 4♠.

Suggested Opening Lead

West leads the ♥8, top of the doubleton in partner's suit.

Declarer's Plan

South's goal is to take at least ten tricks with spades as trumps. There are six sure tricks in spades, one in diamonds, and two in clubs. One more trick is required.

With eight clubs in the combined hands, the club suit provides a chance to develop an extra trick through length.

In considering the order, declarer wants to draw trumps first and then give up a club trick

```
┌─ DECLARER'S PLAN—THE ABC'S ─┐

 Declarer: South    Contract: 4♠

 ASSESS THE SITUATION
 Goal                     10
 Sure Tricks               9
 Extra Tricks Needed       1

 BROWSE DECLARER'S CHECKLIST
 Promotion
 Length                1 in clubs
 The Finesse
 Trumping in dummy

 CONSIDER THE ORDER
  • Draw trumps.
  • Take the loss early in clubs.
```

while still retaining winners in the other suits to regain the lead.

After East wins the first two heart tricks, whatever suit East leads next, declarer can win. South draws trumps, which takes three rounds when the missing trumps are divided 3-1. Declarer next goes after the club suit, playing the ♣A and winning the second trick with dummy's ♣K. A trick can be given up a trick to West's ♣Q. Declarer has now established a low club as a winner.

Comments

When an opponent opens with a preemptive bid, there are two ways to get into the auction: the takeout double and the overcall. On this deal, North-South use an overcall to reach their best contract.

Since East and West are not vulnerable and North-South are vulnerable, East-West might consider sacrificing in 5♥ when North-South reach 4♠. North-South should then make a penalty double. East-West will probably prefer to take their chances defending against 4♠ and hope to defeat it.

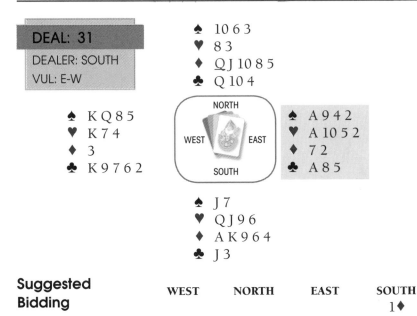

DEAL: 31

DEALER: SOUTH
VUL: E-W

NORTH

♠ 10 6 3
♥ 8 3
♦ Q J 10 8 5
♣ Q 10 4

WEST

♠ K Q 8 5
♥ K 7 4
♦ 3
♣ K 9 7 6 2

EAST

♠ A 9 4 2
♥ A 10 5 2
♦ 7 2
♣ A 8 5

SOUTH

♠ J 7
♥ Q J 9 6
♦ A K 9 6 4
♣ J 3

Suggested Bidding

WEST	NORTH	EAST	SOUTH
			1♦
DOUBLE	3♦	4♦	PASS
4♠	PASS	PASS	PASS

South has 12 high-card points plus 1 length point for the five-card diamond suit. With no five-card major suit, South opens 1♦.

West has a close decision on whether to enter the auction. West has 11 high-card points and could add 1 length point for the five-card club suit. West might overcall 2♣, but the suit isn't very good. With support for the unbid suits, a better choice is to add 3 dummy points for the singleton diamond and make a takeout double.

North, with five-card support for South's suit, can value the hand as 5 high-card points plus 1 dummy point. With 6 points, North could simply raise to 2♦ after West's double but, with such a weak hand, might choose to make a preemptive jump raise to 3♦.

East, as advancer, has 12 high-card points and, since West is showing 13 or more with the takeout double, knows How High, game. East isn't quite as sure about Where. The partnership could belong in 4♥ or 4♠. To get more information, East can cuebid the opponents' suit, 4♦. This is advancer's forcing bid.

After South passes, West would choose 4♠ since West has four spades and only three hearts. West's 4♠ call will likely be followed by three passes, ending the auction with West as declarer.

Suggested Opening Lead

North leads the ♦Q, top of touching honors in the partnership's suit.

Declarer's Plan

West's goal as declarer is to take ten tricks. There are three sure spade tricks, two hearts, and two clubs. Three more tricks are needed.

Declarer browses the checklist. If the five missing spades are divided 3-2, the spade suit will provide an extra trick through length. Similarly, if the five missing clubs are divided 3-2, the club suit will provide two extra tricks through length.

DECLARER'S PLAN—THE ABC'S

Declarer: West   Contract: 4♠

ASSESS THE SITUATION

Goal	10
Sure Tricks	7
Extra Tricks Needed	3

BROWSE DECLARER'S CHECKLIST

Promotion	
Length	1 in spades
	2 in clubs
The Finesse	
Trumping in dummy	

CONSIDER THE ORDER

- Draw trumps first.
- Take the loss early in clubs.

In considering the order, declarer wants to start by drawing the defenders' trumps and then establish the extra club winners early.

Suppose the defenders win the first diamond trick and play a second round of diamonds. West can trump and play the ♠K, ♠Q, and a low spade to the ♠A to draw the defenders' trumps. Then declarer can take the ♣A, ♣K, and lead a third round of clubs to establish West's two remaining clubs as winners. North wins the ♣Q, but whatever suit North leads next, declarer can win and get to the West hand with the ♥K to take the two club winners.

Comments

East could guess whether to bid 4♥ or 4♠ opposite West's takeout double but that could lead to the wrong contract. The cuebid is an effective tool to get the partnership to the best contract when advancer needs more information to decide How High and Where.

DEAL: 32

DEALER: WEST
VUL: BOTH

♠ K 3
♥ K J 3 2
♦ J 7 3 2
♣ 9 5 2

♠ 9 6
♥ 8 6 4
♦ A 8
♣ A Q J 10 8 7

NORTH
WEST   EAST
SOUTH

♠ Q J 10 7 5
♥ 9 5
♦ 10 6 4
♣ K 6 3

♠ A 8 4 2
♥ A Q 10 7
♦ K Q 9 5
♣ 4

Suggested Bidding

WEST	NORTH	EAST	SOUTH
1♣	Pass	1♠	Double
2♣	2♥	Pass	3♥
Pass	4♥	Pass	Pass
Pass			

West is the dealer and has 11 high-card points plus 2 length points for the six-card suit, for a total of 13. West opens 1♣.

North has only 8 high-card points and passes.

East, as responder, has 6 high-card points plus 1 length point for the five-card suit. East bids 1♠, showing 6 or more points and four or more spades.

South has support for both unbid suits, hearts and diamonds. With 15 high-card points and 3 dummy points for the singleton club, South can make a takeout double.

West doesn't have support for spades and doesn't have a balanced hand. West rebids 2♣ to show extra length in the club suit.

North doesn't have to bid after West bids 2♣ but, with 8 points, wants to compete once South invited North into the auction. With four hearts and four diamonds, North bids 2♥, the major suit.

East doesn't have extra for the initial response and passes[53].

---

[53] East might compete to 3♣.

South has 18 points, enough to consider going for the game bonus. South shows a medium-strength hand of about 17–18 points by raising to 3♥. After West passes, North has enough to bid 4♥.

Suggested Opening Lead

East leads the ♣3, low from three or more cards in the suit bid by partner. East might also choose to lead the ♠Q.

Declarer's Plan

North's goal is to take ten tricks. There are two spade tricks and four heart tricks. Four more tricks are needed.

The diamonds provide an opportunity to promote two winners and develop a third trick through length. Since declarer has more clubs than dummy, declarer can also plan to trump two clubs in the dummy to gain two tricks.

In considering the order, declarer wants to keep enough hearts in the dummy to trump

> ┌─ DECLARER'S PLAN—THE ABC'S ─┐
>
> Declarer: North   Contract: 4♥
>
> **A**SSESS THE SITUATION
> | | |
> |---|---|
> | Goal | 10 |
> | Sure Tricks | 6 |
> | Extra Tricks Needed | 4 |
>
> **B**ROWSE DECLARER'S CHECKLIST
> | | |
> |---|---|
> | Promotion | 2 in diamonds |
> | Length | 1 in diamonds |
> | The Finesse | |
> | Trumping in dummy | 2 in clubs |
>
> **C**ONSIDER THE ORDER
> - Leave enough trumps in dummy to trump two clubs.
> - Draw trumps.
> - Take the loss early when promoting tricks in diamonds.

the clubs. Declarer also wants to promote the diamond winners but needs to draw the trumps before taking the established winners.

This is a lot to do, so declarer may not be able to do everything but should still finish with ten tricks. If West wins the first trick with the ♣A and leads a spade, for example, declarer can win and draw three rounds of trumps. Then declarer can promote the diamond winners by giving up a trick to the ♦A. Declarer will have only one trump left in dummy and can trump only one club, but will still have ten tricks.

Comments

Even after West opens the bidding and East responds, North-South can reach their game contract with the help of a takeout double.

Appendices

Appendix 1 – Scoring Formats

Contract bridge can be played with various scoring formats. Three of the most popular are:

- Rubber (social) bridge
- Duplicate (tournament) bridge
- Chicago (four-deal) bridge

The format affects how vulnerability is determined and the way bonuses are awarded.

Rubber Bridge

This format is used when there are only four players or there are several tables and the players want to change partners throughout the session. The length of social games is decided by the players.

The objective in rubber bridge is to be the first partnership to make two games of 100 or more points. A *rubber* is the best two out of three. In rubber bridge, a game can be scored in a single hand or by making two or more partscores that add up to 100 points.

When the rubber begins, both sides are non vulnerable. When a partnership makes a game, it becomes vulnerable and a new game begins. Any partscore the other side has no longer counts toward the next game. When a vulnerable partnership makes its second game, it wins the rubber and receives a bonus (See Appendix 2).

Duplicate Bridge

Duplicate bridge is played in clubs and tournaments, usually with larger groups of players. The players remain in set partnerships throughout the session which lasts for a prearranged period of time, usually 2 to 3½ hours. Each partnership is assigned to a table in either the North-South or East-West direction as indicated by a guide card on each table. The North-South pairs usually stay at the same table throughout the game. The East-West pairs move from table to table after playing a round, a preset number of deals.

The cards are dealt once at the beginning of the game and the four hands are placed in the pockets of a duplicate board. The deal remains intact throughout the game. The dealer and vulnerability are pre-assigned on each board.

At the end of each deal, the partnerships agree on the tricks won or lost and the result of the deal is scored (see Appendix 2). The cards in front of each player are then picked up and placed in the appropriate pocket of the duplicate board, so the same deal can be played at other tables.

Chicago

This format can be used at home or in clubs and is used to avoid long rubbers of uncertain duration. A round, or chukker, of exactly four deals is played. The players can then rearrange the partnerships and play another round.

The cards are shuffled and dealt each time, similar to rubber bridge, with deal moving clockwise around the table. The vulnerability on each deal, however, is predetermined as follows:

First deal: Neither side vulnerable

Second and third deals[55]: Dealer's side vulnerable; other side non-vulnerable.

Fourth deal: Both sides vulnerable

The scoring is a mixture of rubber and duplicate bridge. Game bonuses (see Appendix 2) are awarded immediately and there is no rubber bonus. Partscores, however, carry over from one deal to the next. So, a game bonus can be won by making two or more partscores with a total trick score of 100.

Appendix 2 – Scoring

A partnership scores points in three ways:

- Trick Score
- Bonus Points
- Penalty Points

The trick score and penalty points are the same for all formats of the game, but the bonus points can vary. There are also variations in the score depending on the vulnerability and whether the contract is undoubled, doubled, or redoubled.

Trick Score

A partnership that makes a contract scores points for the tricks bid and made as follows:

	Clubs (♣) or Diamonds (♦)	Hearts (♥) or Spades (♠)	Notrump
First trick	20	30	40
Subsequent tricks	20	30	30

---

[55] The vulnerability on the second and third deals is sometimes reversed.

- The trick score only applies to tricks taken beyond the initial six tricks assumed in the contract.
- If the contract is doubled and made, the trick score is doubled.
- If the contract is redoubled and made, the trick score is quadrupled.

Game is a total trick score of 100 or more points. A game can be scored in a single deal by bidding and making the following contracts:

A contract that is worth less than 100 points is called a *partscore*.

Game Contracts

Game in Notrump	3NT (nine tricks)	40 + 30 + 30 = 100
Game in a Major	4♥ or 4♠ (ten tricks)	30 + 30 + 30 + 30 = 120
Game in a Minor	5♦ or 5♣ (eleven tricks)	20 + 20 + 20 + 20 + 20 = 100

Bonus Points

RUBBER BONUS (RUBBER BRIDGE ONLY)

In rubber bridge, there is no bonus for making a game or partscore unless the rubber is not completed. Instead, after a partnership makes its second game, it wins the rubber and receives:

- 500 if the partnership won the rubber two games to one.
- 700 if the partnership won the rubber two games to none.

If the rubber is not completed, a 300 point bonus is awarded if one side has made a game and a 100 point bonus if one side has made a partscore in an unfinished game.

GAME AND PARTGAME BONUS (DUPLICATE BRIDGE ONLY)

In duplicate bridge, each deal is scored separately. There is no carryover from one deal to the next. The bonuses for bidding and making contracts are awarded as follows:

- 300 for bidding and making a game contract when non vulnerable.
- 500 for bidding and making a game contract when vulnerable.
- 50 for bidding and making a partscore contract.

GAME AND PARTGAME BONUS (CHICAGO BRIDGE ONLY)

In Chicago, a game bonus is awarded when game is made. A partscore bonus is only awarded on the fourth deal:

- 300 for bidding and making a game contract when non vulnerable.
- 500 for bidding and making a game contract when vulnerable.
- 100 for bidding and making a partscore contract on the fourth deal.

SLAM BONUS (ALL FORMATS)

For bidding and making a slam:

	Non Vulnerable	Vulnerable
Small Slam (12 tricks)	500	750
Grand Slam (13 tricks)	1000	1500

OVERTRICKS (ALL FORMATS)

For each trick made in excess of the contract:

	Non Vulnerable	Vulnerable
Undoubled	Trick value	Trick value
Doubled	100	200
Redoubled	200	400

MAKING A DOUBLED OR REDOUBLED CONTRACT (ALL FORMATS)

For making a doubled contract there is a bonus of 50 points. For making a redoubled contract, there is a bonus of 100 points.

HONORS BONUS (RUBBER BRIDGE AND CHICAGO ONLY)

In rubber bridge and Chicago, but not duplicate, an *honors bonus* of 100 points is awarded if a player holds four of the honors in the trump suit and a bonus of 150 points if a player holds all five honors in the trump suit or all four aces in a notrump contract.

Penalty Points

For each trick by which declarer falls short of the contract (*undertrick*):

	Non Vulnerable			Vulnerable		
	Undoubled	Doubled	Redoubled	Undoubled	Doubled	Redoubled
First trick	50	100	200	100	200	400
Second trick	50	200	400	100	300	600
Third and subsequent tricks	50	300	600	100	300	600

Appendix 3—
The Bidding Ladder

BONUS LEVEL
(COMBINED
VALUATION PTS.)

	7NT	
7-Level	7♠	**GRAND**
(13 Tricks)	7♥	**SLAM**
	7♦	**37+**
	7♣	
	6NT	
6-Level	6♠	**SMALL**
(12 Tricks)	6♥	**SLAM**
	6♦	**33+**
	6♣	
	5NT	
5-Level	5♠	
(11 Tricks)	5♥	
	5♦	**GAME**
	5♣	**29+ PTS.**
	4NT	
4-Level	4♠	**GAME**
(10 Tricks)	4♥	**26+ PTS.**
	4♦	
	4♣	
	3NT	**GAME**
3-Level	3♠	**25+ PTS.**
(9 Tricks)	3♥	
	3♦	
	3♣	
	2NT	
2-Level	2♠	
(8 Tricks)	2♥	
	2♦	
	2♣	
	1NT	
1-Level	1♠	
(7 Tricks)	1♥	
	1♦	
	1♣	

BIDDING LADDER

Glossary

Advancer—The partner of a player who makes an overcall or take-out double. (page 54)

Auction—The process of determining the contract through a series of bids. (page 2)

Balanced Hand—A hand with no voids, no singletons, and no more than one doubleton. (page 56)

Bidding Ladder—The order in which bids can be made, starting with 1♣ and ending with 7NT. (page 2)

Bonus—Points scored for making a partscore, game, or slam or for defeating the opponents' contract. (page 4, 216)

Call—Any bid, double, redouble or pass. (page 10)

Chicago—A form of the game which is played in units of four deals. (page 3, 214)

Competitive Auction—An auction in which both sides are bidding to try and win the contract. (page 43)

Competitive Bidding—Entering the auction after the other side has opened the bidding. (page 2)

Combined Hands—Both hands belonging to one partnership. (page 17)

Contract—The undertaking by declarer's side to win at least a specific number of tricks in a specific denomination as determined by the final bid in the auction. (page 1)

Convention—A bid which conveys a meaning other than what would normally be attributed to it. (page 22)

Cuebid (in the Opponents' Suit)—An artificial forcing bid in a suit bid by the opponents. It can be used by responder after an opponent overcalls and by advancer after partner overcalls. (page 59)

Deal—The distribution of the cards to the four players. (page 3)

Declarer—The player from the side that won the auction, who first bid the denomination named in the final contract. (page 3)

Defeat—Stop declarer from making a contract. (page 2)

Defense—The side that did not win the auction. (page 16)

Discard—Play a card to a trick which is from a different suit than the one led and is not a trump. (page 89)

Distribution—The number of cards held in each suit by a particular player; the number of cards held in a particular suit by the partnership. (page 67)

Double—A call that can be used either to ask partner to bid or to increase the bonus for defeating the opponents' contract. (See Negative Double, Takeout Double, Penalty Double.) (page 3)

Doubleton—A holding of two cards in a suit. (page 54)

Draw Trump—Playing the trump suit until the opponents have none left. (page 26)

Dummy Points—Points used in place of length points when valuing a hand in support of partner's suit: void, 5 points; singleton, 3 points; doubleton, 1 point. (page 54)

Duplicate—A form of the game in which the same deal is played more than once. (page 3, 214)

Establish—Set up sure tricks by driving out winning cards in the opponents' hands. (page 18)

Feature—A potentially useful high card, such as an ace or a king, in a suit. A feature can be shown after opening a weak two-bid when responder uses the artificial 2NT response. (page 22)

Finesse—A method of building extra tricks by trapping an opponent's high card(s). (page 25)

Fit—Ideally, three-card or longer support for a suit bid by partner. A combined partnership holding of eight or more cards in a suit will usually be a suitable trump fit. (page 11)

Forcing (Bid)—A bid that partner is not expected to pass. (page 13)

Fourth Highest—A lead of the fourth card down from the top in a suit. (page 41)

Game—A total trick score of 100 or more points. (page 4, 216)

Game Contract—A contract which has a trick score value of 100 or more points. (page 4, 216)

Go Down—Be defeated in a contract. For example, 'down three' would indicate that the contract was defeated by three tricks. (page 5)

Grand Slam—A contract to take all thirteen tricks. (page 217)

Guideline of 500—See Rule of 500. (page 6)

Guideline of Two and Three—See Rule of 500. (page 6)

Hand Valuation—The method to determine the value of a particular hand during the auction. Usually a combination of high card strength and suit length or shortness. (page 46)

HCPs—An abbreviation for high-card points. (page 1)

High Card—One of the top four cards in a suit: ace, king, queen, or jack. (page 1)

High Card Points—The value of high cards in a hand: ace, 4; king, 3; queen, 2; jack, 1. (page 1)

Higher-Ranking Suit—A suit that ranks higher on the Bidding Ladder than another suit. Spades are ranked highest; hearts are second; diamonds are third; clubs are the lowest-ranking suit. (page 49)

Honor (Card)—An ace, king, queen, jack or ten. (page 8)

How High—The level at which the contract should be played. (page 7)

Invitational—A bid which encourages partner to continue bidding. (page 67)

Jump Overcall—An overcall at a level higher than necessary. For example, 2♠ would be a jump overcall over an opening bid of 1♥ because it is only necessary to bid 1♠. A jump overcall is typically used as a preemptive bid. (page 72)

Length Points—The valuation assigned to long suits in a hand: five-card suit, 1 point; six-card suit, 2 points; seven-card suit, 3 points; eight-card suit, 4 points. (page 2)

Loser—A trick which might be lost to the opponents. (page 23)

Major (Suit)—Spades or hearts. (page 4)

Minor (Suit)—Diamonds or clubs. (page 4)

Negative Double (Responder's Double)—A takeout double by responder after partner opens one of a suit and the next player overcalls in a suit. (page 144)

New Suit—A suit which has not previously been bid in the auction. (page 10)

Non Vulnerable—In rubber bridge, a partnership that has not won a game. In duplicate or Chicago scoring, the vulnerability is assigned to each deal. The bonuses and penalties are less when a partnership is non vulnerable than when it is vulnerable. (page 3, 214)

Obstructive Bid—A bid intended to make it more challenging for the opponents to find their best contract. (page 7)

One Level—The lowest level at which the auction can start. It represents seven tricks. (page 1)

Opening Lead—The card led to the first trick. The player to declarer's left leads first. (page 23)

Overbid—A bid for more tricks than can reasonably be expected to be taken. Typically used in competitive auctions to make it more challenging for the opponents to find their best contract. (page 6)

Overcall—A bid made after the opponents have opened the bidding. (page 43)

Overtrick—A trick won by declarer in excess of the number required to make the contract. (page 85, 217)

Partscore—A contract that does not receive a game bonus if made. (page 216)

Pattern—The number of cards held in each suit in a player's hand. (page 94)

Penalty—The bonus awarded to the defenders for defeating a contract. (page 3, 218)

Penalty Double—A double made with the expectation of defeating the opponents' contract. Partner is expected to pass. (page 3, 160)

Playing Tricks—Tricks a hand can be expected to take if the partnership buys the contract. (page 1)

Preemptive Jump Raise—A raise of partner's suit one or more levels higher than necessary to show a weak hand with good trump support. Typically used by responder after right-hand opponent overcalls or makes a takeout double, or by advancer after partner overcalls in a suit. (page 56)

Preemptive Opening Bid—An opening bid in a suit of 2♦ or higher. Preemptive opening bids describe a weak hand with a good long suit and are designed to make it more challenging for the opponents to enter the auction. (page 2)

Promotion—Developing one or more cards into winners by driving out any higher-ranking cards held by the opponents. (page 24)

Rank of the Suits—The suits are ranked in order during the bidding: spades are highest, then hearts, diamonds and clubs. Notrump ranks higher than spades. (page 49)

Raise—Supporting partner's suit by bidding the suit at a higher level. (page 10)

Rebid—A second bid by the same player. (page 14)

Redouble—A call that increases the bonuses for making or defeating a contract that has already been doubled. It can be used by responder to show about 10 or more points after the opening bid is doubled. (page 148, 218)

Responder—The partner of the opening bidder. (page 7)

Responder's Double—See Negative Double. (page 144)

Rubber—The unit of play in rubber bridge which ends when one partnership wins two games. (page 213)

Rubber Bonus—The bonus awarded for winning the rubber when playing rubber bridge. (page 216)

Rubber Bridge—One of the popular forms of contract bridge. (page 3, 213)

Ruff(ing)—Play a trump to a trick when holding no cards in the suit led. Same as trumping. (page 26)

Rule of 500—A guideline on how much a partnership can afford to overbid on the assumption the contract will be doubled but the opponents can make at least a game contract. When vulnerable, the guideline is to overbid by two tricks because the penalty for being doubled and down two is 500 points; when non vulnerable, the guideline is to overbid by three tricks because the penalty for being doubled and down three is 500 points. (page 6)

Rule of Two and Three—See Rule of 500. (page 6)

Sacrifice—Deliberately overbidding to a contract that is not expected to make in the hope that the penalty will be less than the value of the opponents' potential contract. (page 6)

Sequence—Three or more consecutive cards in a suit. (page 35)

Short Side—The partnership hand with the fewer cards in a specific suit. (page 26)

Signoff (Bid)—A bid that asks partner to pass. (page 13)

Simple Overcall—A non-jump overcall; an overcall at the cheapest available level. (page 44)

Singleton—A holding of one card in a suit. (page 54)

Slam—A contract to take twelve or thirteen tricks. (page 12)

Small Slam—A contract to take twelve tricks. (page 217)

Strength—The value of a hand in terms of its high-card points and length or dummy points. (page 1)

Support—The number of cards held in a suit that partner has bid. (page 12)

Sure Trick—A trick which can be taken without giving up the lead to the opponents. (page 11)

Takeout Double—A double that asks partner to bid an unbid suit. (page 92)

Trick Score—The points scored for contracts bid and made. (page 4, 215)

Trumping—Playing a trump on a trick when void in the suit led. (page 26)

Two Level—The second level on the Bidding Ladder. It represents eight tricks. (page 44)

Unbalanced Hand—A hand with a void, a singleton, or more than one doubleton. (page 55)

Unbid Suit—A suit that has not yet been bid during the auction. (page 92)

Undertrick—Each trick by which declarer's side fails to fulfill the contract. (page 218)

Undoubled—A contract that has not been doubled by the opponents. (page 5)

Up the Line—Bidding the cheapest of two or more four-card suits (page 111)

Valuation (Points)—A method of estimating the value of a hand during the auction, usually a combination of values for high cards and length. (page 46)

Void—A holding of zero cards in a suit. (page 54)

Vulnerable—In rubber bridge, a partnership that has won a game. In duplicate or Chicago scoring, the vulnerability is assigned to each deal. The bonuses and penalties are greater when a partnership is vulnerable than when it is non vulnerable. (page 3, 214)

Vulnerability—The status of the hand during a round of bridge which affects the size of the bonuses awarded for making or defeating contracts. (page 3, 214)

Where—The strain (clubs, diamonds, hearts, spades, or notrump) in which the contract should be played. (page 7)

Winner—A card held by one of the players that will win a trick when it is played. (page 23)

Audrey Grant
www.AudreyGrant.com

I'd like to invite you to subscribe to **Better Bridge**, a bi-monthly, 24 page magazine for everyone who loves the game of bridge. Whether you play at home, at the club or in tournaments, you will find the **Better Bridge** magazine to be timely, insightful and thoroughly enjoyable. Each issue is full of useful information brought to you by the world's best players and writers; the up-to-date tips will have you playing better bridge!

AUDREY GRANT'S Better Bridge
• A magazine for all bridge players •

**$29/YEAR U.S.
for 6 issues**

SAVE $13 OFF THE SINGLE ISSUE PRICE

BARON BARCLAY BRIDGE SUPPLIES
3600 Chamberlain Lane, Suite 230
Louisville, KY 40241   FAX: 502-426-2044
www.baronbarclay.com

1-800-274-2221
TOLL FREE IN THE U.S. & CANADA

Visit our web site to get
up-to-date information from Better Bridge.

www.BetterBridge.com OR www.AudreyGrant.com

PRODUCTS

Better Bridge material is prepared with the assistance of the Better Bridge Panel of world-wide experts and is available through books, disks, videos, magazines, and the Internet.

BRIDGE TEACHERS

Join the Better Bridge Teachers' Group if you are involved in bridge education. Teacher's manuals are available to assist in presenting bridge lessons to students.

CRUISES

Travel by ship, add Bridge at Sea, and you have a magic fit. Audrey Grant and the Better Bridge Team conduct bridge cruises to locations around the world.

FESTIVALS

Workshops and festivals are held in fine hotels and resorts across North America. Come with or without a partner . . . let us get a fourth for bridge.

BRIDGE QUIZ

Try the regularly updated quizzical pursuits. Test your bidding and play, spot the celebrities, and play detective at the table.

BRIDGE ONLINE

Playing bridge on the internet is becoming an increasingly popular pastime since you can play anywhere, anytime. Find out about the Audrey Grant bridge club and lessons.

CONTACT US

E-mail:	BetterBridge@BetterBridge.com
Phone:	1-888-266-4447
Fax:	1-416-322-6601
Write:	Better Bridge
	247 Wanless Avenue
	Toronto, ON M4N 1W5